SWEETSPOT PLANNER
90 DAYS TO LIVE | LOVE | LEARN | LEAD
ACCORDING TO THE CALL GOD HAS ON YOUR LIFE

The Legacy Series

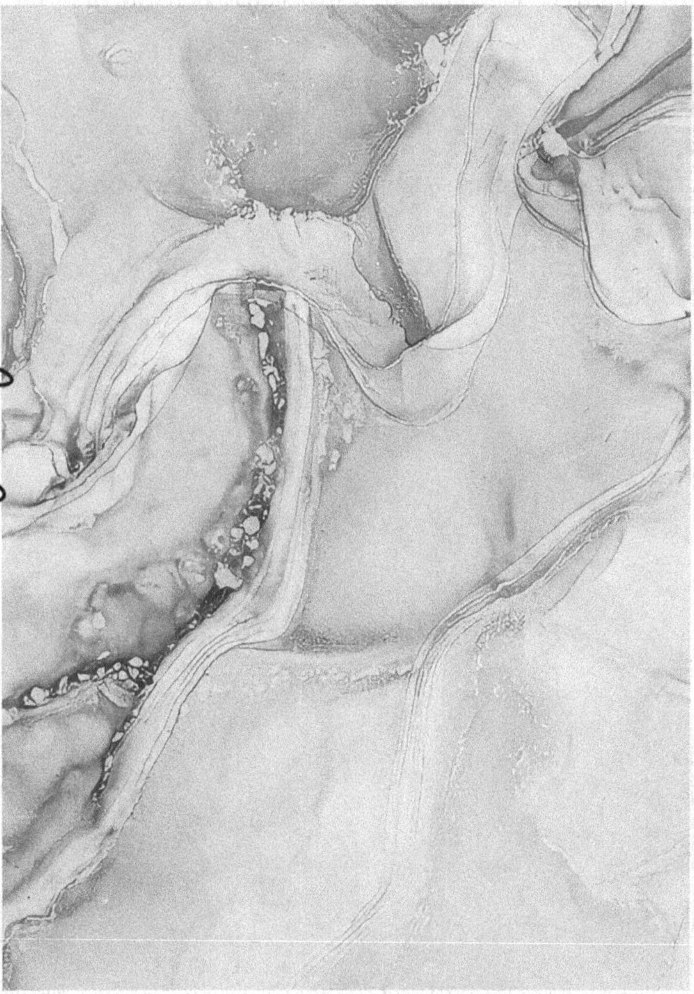

BY NICCIE KLIEGL

Sweetspot Planner © 2022 by Niccie Kliegl. All rights reserved.

All rights reserved. This book contains material protected under International and Federal Copyright Laws and Treaties. Any unauthorized reprint or use of this material is prohibited. No part of this book may be reproduced or transmitted in any form or by any means, electronic or mechanical, including photocopying, recording, or by any information storage and retrieval system, without express written permission from the author.

ISBN: 978-1-7387721-0-0 (paperback)
ISBN: 978-1-7387721-1-7 (hardcover)

Available in paperback and hardcover

Unless otherwise noted, all Scripture quotations are taken from the English Standard Version. Biblica, 2001 Bible Gateway.com, www.biblegateway.com/versions/The Holy Bible, English Standard Version – ASV-Bible/#booklist

Published by Reachout Publishing
PO Box 159, Clyde, Alberta T0G 0P0
www.reachloveconnect.com

table of CONTENTS

01
WELCOME (LEGACY SERIES & FREE GIFTS)

02
YOUR GOAL SETTING

03
YOUR SABBATH STYLE SYSTEM (DAILY SHEETS)

04
YOUR SUCCESS (MONTHLY SHEETS)

05
JOIN THE LEGACY LEADER COMMUNITY

NICCIEKLIEGL.COM

The Legacy Series

The Sweetspot Planner is based on my 4-part life coaching book series *The Legacy Series*. While coaching on these four faith-based programs I witnessed marriages restored, abuse and addiction healed, life purpose found, and the list goes on. Getting God-partnered and *Tapping into the Trinity*© transforms lives. Once we get into our sweetspot we want to share it with others; in our home, the community, and eventually the nations. I now lead the Legacy Leader Community who lives and works within their Sweetspot. They all have their stories that God has transformed and blessed. There is nothing too messy for God to turn into good. (John 10:10)

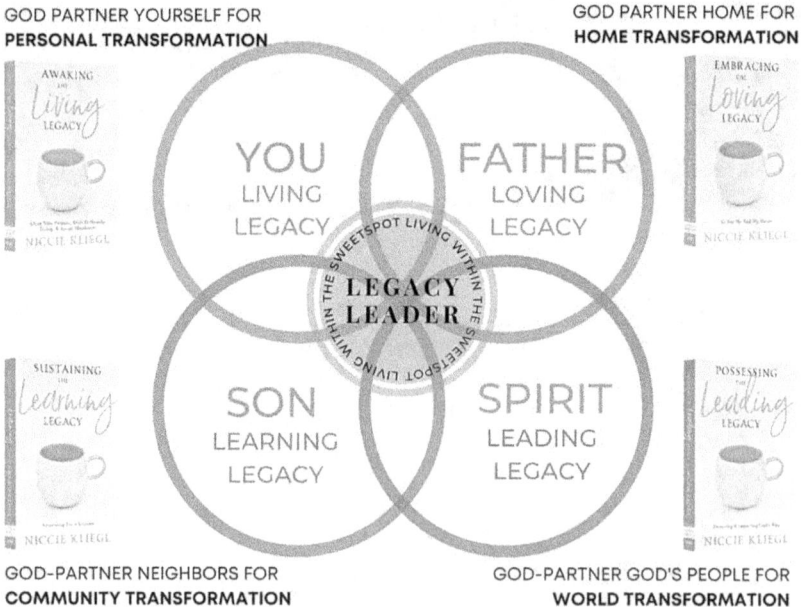

Use the QR code to get a copy of *The Legacy Series* books today. And please head to my website at niccickliegl.com to learn more about the sweetspot, our commmunity, and programs.

Get your FREE RESOURCES

3-DAY FORTIFY YOUR PRAYER MINI-COURSE

JOIN THE BIBLE IN A YEAR PROGRAM

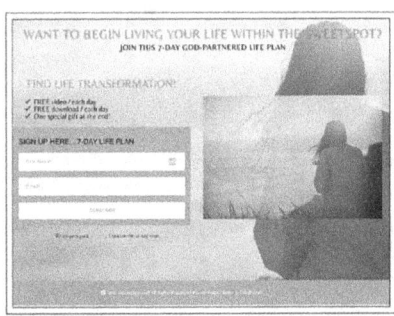

7-DAY GOD-PARTNERED LIFE BALANCE

BOOK A FREE SWEETSPOT SESSION

Fulfill Your Legacy | nicciekliegl.com | Life & Business Coach

FULFILL YOUR LEGACY

PRAY
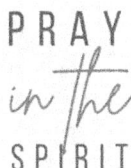
in the
SPIRIT

And pray in the Spirit on all occasions with all kinds of prayers and requests. With this in mind, be alert and always keep on praying for all the Lord's people. Ephesians 6:18

Keep a list here of who/what you want to pray for regularly.
Pray confidently knowing you are one with Christ - the Lord - IN THE SPIRIT. He can, will, and wants to hear from you and support you. When you do not know what to say HE (the Holy Spirit) knows.

Welcome
01

I am an author, life and business coach, and speaker who elevates others into their SWEETSPOT, where they get more out of life and work because they partner with God, know their divine purpose, and tap into all the Trinity offers. **Here, they fulfill their legacy... they live, love, learn, and lead according to the call God has on their lives!**

I spent 20+ years in my dream job and one day found myself knowing I was supposed to do something more. I had no idea what it was, but God did. For the first time in my life, I tapped into Him and started getting answers. Now I help thousands of others do the same. Whether you are an individual looking for life purpose or feeling like there has to be more to life or if you are a faith-based entrepreneur feeling frustrated or held back in your business start-up or next level...God has the answers and I'd like to help.

This planner is used by thousands of my clients to help them get into their SWEETSPOT so their life and business are God-partnered and succeeding.

xoxo Niccie

Goal Setting
02

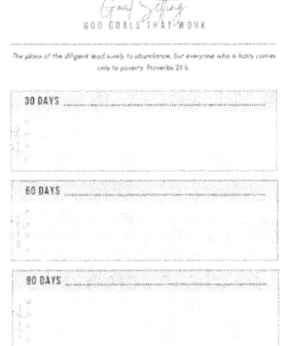

Goal setting is so necessary for making advancements in life and business which is why you will find some wonderful tools to help you make what I call... GOD GOALS.

(Please use this code to take my **FREE God Goals Mini-course** if you'd like to get really God-partnered in your goals and the call God has on your life.)

We can achieve great things on our own with SMART goals but in order to truly partner God with your goals and actions I'm including four essential tools that I use with both my life and business clients.

- Let's Assess: This should just get you thinking about what you are or aren't currently doing. Then it should nudge you toward a new goal.
- Let's Prioritize: This is transforming. So try to delegate & dump one item each month until you find yourself doing life within your SWEETSPOT.
- S.M.A.R.T. Goals: We know that these 5 steps are crucial so I gave you a tool to hold you to it. Now go make smart goals.
- Goal Setting: Commit your goals to paper (even email me a screenshot at niccie@nicciekliegl.com) so I can support you!

Let's Assess
HUMBLE AWARENESS LEAVES ROOM FOR GOD

For by the grace given to me I say to everyone among you not to think of himself more highly than he ought to think, but to think with sober judgment, each according to the measure of faith that God has assigned. Romans 12:3 ESV

HOW DO YOU RATE THE FOLLOWING?

Physically

	NEVER	RARELY	SOMETIMES	ALWAYS
I FEEL GOOD ABOUT MY BODY	○	○	○	○
I EXERCISE TO KEEP MY BODY HEALTHY	○	○	○	○
I GET 7-8 HOURS OF SLEEP EVERY DAY	○	○	○	○
I CHOOSE NUTRITIOUS FOOD OVER PROCESSED	○	○	○	○
I GET 8, 8 OUNCE GLASSES OF WATER/DAY	○	○	○	○

HOW DO YOU RATE THE FOLLOWING?

Spiritually

	NEVER	RARELY	SOMETIMES	ALWAYS
I SPEND TIME IN THE BIBLE AND THE WORD	○	○	○	○
I TAP INTO THE TRINITY FOR STRENGTH & PEACE	○	○	○	○
I HAVE A SOLID PRAYER LIFE	○	○	○	○
I HAVE A COMMUNITY OF WISE COUNSEL	○	○	○	○

HOW DO YOU RATE THE FOLLOWING?

Mentally

	NEVER	RARELY	SOMETIMES	ALWAYS
I DO NOT CONSUME USELESS PROGRAMMING	○	○	○	○
I MEDITATE ON SCRIPTURE/PRAISE MUSIC DAILY	○	○	○	○
I AM AWARE AND REBUKE SPIRITUAL WARFARE	○	○	○	○

Let's Prioritize
DO IT | DELEGATE IT | DUMP IT

It's important to do things that are in your SWEETSPOT. God made you unique and others as well. Sometimes we waste time, energy, and love for whom God made us to be by doing things we shouldn't, or things we should lean on a community for. Consider dumping or deligating things that are landing in the bottom two fields.

LOVE IT | LIKE IT

DISLIKE IT | HATE IT

FULFILL YOUR LEGACY | NICCIEKLIEGL.COM | LIFE & BUSINESS COACH

FULFILL YOUR LEGACY

Smart Goals
USE THIS TO HELP ACHIEVE YOUR GOALS

For which of you, desiring to build a tower, does not first sit down and count the cost, whether he has enough to complete it?
Luke 14:28 ESV

S	**SPECIFIC** WHAT DO I WANT TO ACCOMPLISH?	
M	**MEASURABLE** HOW WILL I KNOW WHEN IT IS ACCOMPLISHED?	
A	**ACHIEVABLE** HOW CAN THE GOAL BE ACCOMPLISHED?	
R	**RELEVANT** DOES THIS SEEM WORTHWHILE?	
T	**TIME BOUND** WHEN CAN I ACCOMPLISH THIS GOAL?	

FULFILL YOUR LEGACY | NICCIEKLIEGL.COM | LIFE & BUSINESS COACH
FULFILL **YOUR** LEGACY

Goal Setting
GOD GOALS THAT WORK

The plans of the diligent lead surely to abundance, but everyone who is hasty comes only to poverty. Proverbs 21:5 ESV

30 DAYS ....

action plan
- ○
- ○
- ○
- ○

60 DAYS ....

action plan
- ○
- ○
- ○
- ○

90 DAYS ....

action plan
- ○
- ○
- ○
- ○

Sabbath Style System
03

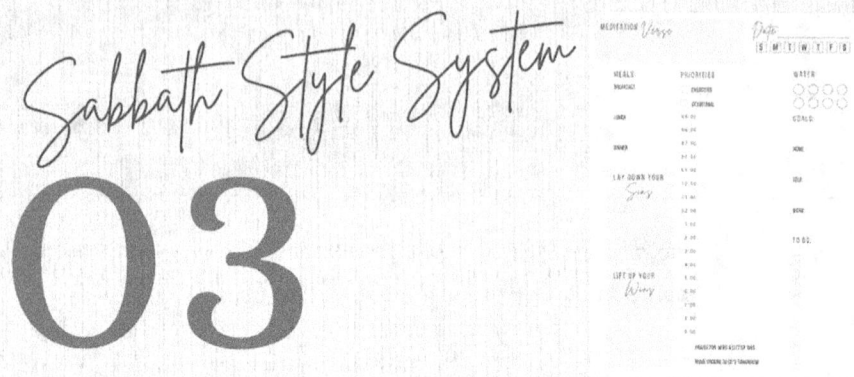

This daily tool inspired the *SWEETSPOT Planner* and my private mastermind. We used this form daily, meeting weekly (Sabbath Style), to reflect on how God-partnered our living was. ONE BY ONE our lives transformed through its prompting to:
- Commit to healthy meal planning.
- Track our water consumption.
- Keep health, life, and work goals alive in our minds
- Meditate on verses using our 4-Part Legacy Process:

CONSIDER THE PROBLEM - 'difficulty' you're experiencing
CONSIDER THE WORD - use the internet to look up verses on your issue, read them, and choose one to meditate on.
CONSIDER THE GIFT - right out the gift you see by doing or believing what the bible verse is saying (this increases faith).
CONSIDER THE CHOICE - w/ free-will decide if you'll lay down your difficulty, find biblical truth, meditate on it, and let God do the transforming work needed to elevate your life.

This powerful daily sheet also includes:
- Cues to repent daily so Satan cannot get a foothold on us.
- Cues to praise daily so we can see God's work in our life.
- A spot for daily timeline/organization, decreasing chaos.
- A spot for your to-do list as well as cues to move uncompleted items to the next day (no more procrastinating)!

FULFILL YOUR LEGACY | NICCIEKLIEGL.COM | LIFE & BUSINESS COACH
FULFILL YOUR LEGACY

Success Planning & Tracking

04

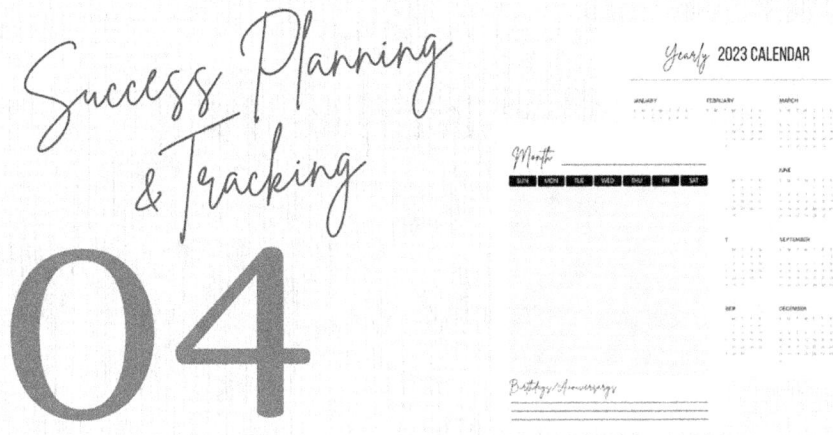

Goal setting and planning for the day, week, month, and year is important, but I believe it's the tracking that sets us up for true success.

So often we forget important dates, inadvertently planning something exciting and new over a reoccurring event, or we run around crazy, stressfully reacting to this busy world.

- Taking 10 minutes at the start of each month to record your routine and important monthly events is priceless.
- Having one place to go to at the end of the year makes tax time a breeze. So keep your planner with one envelope of receipts per planner. You'll be set at the end of the year.
- Use the quick reference yearly calendar(s) to plan for the future and utilize the space at the bottom of your monthly calendar to keep future events rolling over from month to month. This too will keep you from double booking in future months.
- Also, feel free to buy several of these planners. Many of my coaching clients do this, getting their year's appointments all mapped out early. *PLANNING AHEAD WITH THIS PLANNER EQUALS SUCCESS.

Yearly 2023 CALENDAR

JANUARY

S	M	T	W	T	F	S
1	2	3	4	5	6	7
8	9	10	11	12	13	14
15	16	17	18	19	20	21
22	23	24	25	26	27	28
29	30	31				

FEBRUARY

S	M	T	W	T	F	S
			1	2	3	4
5	6	7	8	9	10	11
12	13	14	15	16	17	18
19	20	21	22	23	24	25
26	27	28				

MARCH

S	M	T	W	T	F	S
			1	2	3	4
5	6	7	8	9	10	11
12	13	14	15	16	17	18
19	20	21	22	23	24	25
26	27	28	29	30	31	

APRIL

S	M	T	W	T	F	S
						1
2	3	4	5	6	7	8
9	10	11	12	13	14	15
16	17	18	19	20	21	22
23	24	25	26	27	28	29
30						

MAY

S	M	T	W	T	F	S
	1	2	3	4	5	6
7	8	9	10	11	12	13
14	15	16	17	18	19	20
21	22	23	24	25	26	27
28	29	30	31			

JUNE

S	M	T	W	T	F	S
				1	2	3
4	5	6	7	8	9	10
11	12	13	14	15	16	17
18	19	20	21	22	23	24
25	26	27	28	29	30	

JULY

S	M	T	W	T	F	S
						1
2	3	4	5	6	7	8
9	10	11	12	13	14	15
16	17	18	19	20	21	22
23	24	25	26	27	28	29
30	31					

AUGUST

S	M	T	W	T	F	S
		1	2	3	4	5
6	7	8	9	10	11	12
13	14	15	16	17	18	19
20	21	22	23	24	25	26
27	28	29	30	31		

SEPTEMBER

S	M	T	W	T	F	S
					1	2
3	4	5	6	7	8	9
10	11	12	13	14	15	16
17	18	19	20	21	22	23
24	25	26	27	28	29	30

OCTOBER

S	M	T	W	T	F	S
1	2	3	4	5	6	7
8	9	10	11	12	13	14
15	16	17	18	19	20	21
22	23	24	25	26	27	28
29	30	31				

NOVEMBER

S	M	T	W	T	F	S
			1	2	3	4
5	6	7	8	9	10	11
12	13	14	15	16	17	18
19	20	21	22	23	24	25
26	27	28	29	30		

DECEMBER

S	M	T	W	T	F	S
					1	2
3	4	5	6	7	8	9
10	11	12	13	14	15	16
17	18	19	20	21	22	23
24	25	26	27	28	29	30
31						

Quick View YEARLY CALENDARS

2023 2024

2025 2026

Notes _____

Notes

Month _____

SUN	MON	TUE	WED	THU	FRI	SAT

BIRTHDAYS/ANNIVERSARIES

_____
_____
_____

FUTURE EVENTS TO CARRY OVER

_____
_____
_____

FULFILL YOUR LEGACY | NICCIEKLIEGL.COM | LIFE & BUSINESS COACH

FULFILL YOUR LEGACY

Budget

MONTHLY BALANCE GOAL: _____

INCOME

DATE	SOURCE	CATEGORY	AMOUNT

BILLS & FIXED EXPENSES

DATE	SOURCE	AMOUNT

VARIABLE EXPENSES

DATE	SOURCE	AMOUNT

SUMMARY

SOURCE	AMOUNT
INCOME	
BILLS & FIXED EXPENSES	
VARIABLE EXPENSES	
BALANCE	

FULFILL YOUR LEGACY | NICCIEKLIEGL.COM | LIFE & BUSINESS COACH

FULFILL YOUR LEGACY

MEDITATION *Verse*

(REWRITE YESTERDAY'S PROBLEM-WORD-GIFT-CHOICE MEMORY VERSE HERE)

Date: _____

| S | M | T | W | T | F | S |

MEALS:
BREAKFAST

LUNCH

DINNER

LAY DOWN YOUR *Sins*

LIFT UP YOUR *Wins*

PRIORITIES:
- [ ] EXERCISED
- [ ] DEVOTIONS & JOURNAL COMPLETED

- 05:00
- 06:00
- 07:00
- 08:00
- 09:00
- 10:00
- 11:00
- 12:00
- 1:00
- 2:00
- 3:00
- 4:00
- 5:00
- 6:00
- 7:00
- 8:00
- 9:00

- [ ] PRAY FOR TODAY, HIS COVERING AS YOU SLEEP, AND HIS PRESENCE TOMORROW
- [ ] MOVE UNDONE TO-DO'S TO TOMORROW

WATER:
○ ○ ○ ○
○ ○ ○ ○

GOALS:

HOME:

SELF:

WORK:

TO DO:
- [ ]
- [ ]
- [ ]
- [ ]
- [ ]
- [ ]
- [ ]
- [ ]
- [ ]
- [ ]
- [ ]
- [ ]
- [ ]
- [ ]

Journal
RECORD NUDGES FROM DAILY DEVOTION

The Legacy Leaders like to use a popular process of P.R.A.Y. (pause, rejoice, ask, yield) after their daily Devo. As things come to you trust that it is the Holy Spirit nudging you and then do PROBLEM/WORD/GIFT/CHOICE to tap into God's help.

FREE JOURNALING OF WHATEVER IS ON YOUR MIND AS YOU THINK, LISTEN, OR WHAT WEIGHS ON YOUR MIND:

....
....
....

P (PAUSE)
....

R (REJOICE)
....

A (ASK)
....

Y (YIELD)
....

WAS THERE ANYTHING YOU FELT NUDGED TO WORK ON? LET'S TAP INTO THE WORD FOR HELP

PROBLEM (EXAMPLES ARE WORRY, FEAR, DOUBT, INSECURITY, IMPATIENCE)
....

WORD (GO TO THE INTERNET & LOOK UP 'MEMORY VERSES ON YOUR TOPIC & RECORD A FEW HERE)
....
....
....

GIFT (WRITE ABOUT WHAT LIFE WOULD LIKE BE IF YOU FOLLOW THE WORD)
....

CHOICE (YOU HAVE FREE WILL. WRITE OUT HOW YOU PLAN TO FOLLOW THROUGH)
....

MEDITATION *Verse*

(REWRITE YESTERDAY'S PROBLEM-WORD-GIFT-CHOICE MEMORY VERSE HERE)

Date: _____

| S | M | T | W | T | F | S |

MEALS:

BREAKFAST

LUNCH

DINNER

LAY DOWN YOUR *Sins*

LIFT UP YOUR *Wins*

PRIORITIES:

☐ EXERCISED
☐ DEVOTIONS & JOURNAL COMPLETED

- 05:00
- 06:00
- 07:00
- 08:00
- 09:00
- 10:00
- 11:00
- 12:00
- 1:00
- 2:00
- 3:00
- 4:00
- 5:00
- 6:00
- 7:00
- 8:00
- 9:00

☐ PRAY FOR TODAY, HIS COVERING AS YOU SLEEP, AND HIS PRESENCE TOMORROW
☐ MOVE UNDONE TO-DO'S TO TOMORROW

WATER:
○ ○ ○ ○
○ ○ ○ ○

GOALS:

HOME:

SELF:

WORK:

TO DO:

☐
☐
☐
☐
☐
☐
☐
☐
☐
☐
☐
☐
☐
☐
☐

Journal
RECORD NUDGES FROM DAILY DEVOTION

The Legacy Leaders like to use a popular process of P.R.A.Y. (pause, rejoice, ask, yield) after their daily Devo. As things come to you trust that it is the Holy Spirit nudging you and then do PROBLEM/WORD/GIFT/CHOICE to tap into God's help.

FREE JOURNALING OF WHATEVER IS ON YOUR MIND AS YOU THINK, LISTEN, OR WHAT WEIGHS ON YOUR MIND:

....
....
....

P (PAUSE)
....

R (REJOICE)
....

A (ASK)
....

Y (YIELD)
....
....

WAS THERE ANYTHING YOU FELT NUDGED TO WORK ON? LET'S TAP INTO THE WORD FOR HELP

PROBLEM (EXAMPLES ARE WORRY, FEAR, DOUBT, INSECURITY, IMPATIENCE)
....

WORD (GO TO THE INTERNET & LOOK UP 'MEMORY VERSES ON YOUR TOPIC & RECORD A FEW HERE)
....
....
....

GIFT (WRITE ABOUT WHAT LIFE WOULD LIKE BE IF YOU FOLLOW THE WORD)
....

CHOICE (YOU HAVE FREE WILL, WRITE OUT HOW YOU PLAN TO FOLLOW THROUGH)
....

MEDITATION *Verse*

Date: _____

| S | M | T | W | T | F | S |

(REWRITE YESTERDAY'S PROBLEM-WORD-GIFT-CHOICE MEMORY VERSE HERE)

MEALS:

BREAKFAST

LUNCH

DINNER

PRIORITIES:

☐ EXERCISED
☐ DEVOTIONS & JOURNAL COMPLETED

05:00
06:00
07:00
08:00
09:00
10:00
11:00
12:00
1:00
2:00
3:00
4:00
5:00
6:00
7:00
8:00
9:00

☐ PRAY FOR TODAY, HIS COVERING AS YOU SLEEP, AND HIS PRESENCE TOMORROW
☐ MOVE UNDONE TO-DO'S TO TOMORROW

WATER:
○ ○ ○ ○
○ ○ ○ ○

GOALS:

HOME:

SELF:

WORK:

TO DO:
☐
☐
☐
☐
☐
☐
☐
☐
☐
☐
☐
☐
☐

LAY DOWN YOUR *Sins*

LIFT UP YOUR *Wins*

Journal
RECORD NUDGES FROM DAILY DEVOTION

The Legacy Leaders like to use a popular process of P.R.A.Y. (pause, rejoice, ask, yield) after their daily Devo. As things come to you trust that it is the Holy Spirit nudging you and then do PROBLEM/WORD/GIFT/CHOICE to tap into God's help.

FREE JOURNALING OF WHATEVER IS ON YOUR MIND AS YOU THINK, LISTEN, OR WHAT WEIGHS ON YOUR MIND:

....

....

....

P (PAUSE)
....

R (REJOICE)
....

A (ASK)
....

Y (YIELD)
....

....

WAS THERE ANYTHING YOU FELT NUDGED TO WORK ON? LET'S TAP INTO THE WORD FOR HELP

PROBLEM (EXAMPLES ARE WORRY, FEAR, DOUBT, INSECURITY, IMPATIENCE) ....

WORD (GO TO THE INTERNET & LOOK UP 'MEMORY VERSES ON YOUR TOPIC & RECORD A FEW HERE)

....

....

GIFT (WRITE ABOUT WHAT LIFE WOULD LIKE BE IF YOU FOLLOW THE WORD)
....

CHOICE (YOU HAVE FREE WILL, WRITE OUT HOW YOU PLAN TO FOLLOW THROUGH)
....

MEDITATION *Verse*

(REWRITE YESTERDAY'S PROBLEM-WORD-GIFT-CHOICE MEMORY VERSE HERE)

Date: _____

| S | M | T | W | T | F | S |

MEALS:

BREAKFAST

LUNCH

DINNER

PRIORITIES:

- [ ] EXERCISED
- [ ] DEVOTIONS & JOURNAL COMPLETED

05:00
06:00
07:00
08:00
09:00
10:00
11:00
12:00
1:00
2:00
3:00
4:00
5:00
6:00
7:00
8:00
9:00

WATER:
○ ○ ○ ○
○ ○ ○ ○

GOALS:

HOME:

SELF:

WORK:

TO DO:
- [ ]
- [ ]
- [ ]
- [ ]
- [ ]
- [ ]
- [ ]
- [ ]
- [ ]
- [ ]
- [ ]
- [ ]
- [ ]
- [ ]
- [ ]

LAY DOWN YOUR *Sins*

LIFT UP YOUR *Wins*

- [ ] PRAY FOR TODAY, HIS COVERING AS YOU SLEEP, AND HIS PRESENCE TOMORROW
- [ ] MOVE UNDONE TO-DO'S TO TOMORROW

Journal
RECORD NUDGES FROM DAILY DEVOTION

The Legacy Leaders like to use a popular process of P.R.A.Y. (pause, rejoice, ask, yield) after their daily Devo. As things come to you trust that it is the Holy Spirit nudging you and then do PROBLEM/WORD/GIFT/CHOICE to tap into God's help.

FREE JOURNALING OF WHATEVER IS ON YOUR MIND AS YOU THINK, LISTEN, OR WHAT WEIGHS ON YOUR MIND:

....
....
....

P (PAUSE)
....

R (REJOICE)
....

A (ASK)
....

Y (YIELD)
....
....

WAS THERE ANYTHING YOU FELT NUDGED TO WORK ON? LET'S TAP INTO THE WORD FOR HELP

PROBLEM (EXAMPLES ARE WORRY, FEAR, DOUBT, INSECURITY, IMPATIENCE)
....

WORD (GO TO THE INTERNET & LOOK UP 'MEMORY VERSES ON YOUR TOPIC & RECORD A FEW HERE)
....
....
....

GIFT (WRITE ABOUT WHAT LIFE WOULD LIKE BE IF YOU FOLLOW THE WORD)
....

CHOICE (YOU HAVE FREE WILL, WRITE OUT HOW YOU PLAN TO FOLLOW THROUGH)
....
....

MEDITATION *Verse*

(REWRITE YESTERDAY'S PROBLEM-WORD-GIFT-CHOICE MEMORY VERSE HERE)

Date: _____

| S | M | T | W | T | F | S |

MEALS:

BREAKFAST

LUNCH

DINNER

PRIORITIES:

☐ EXERCISED
☐ DEVOTIONS & JOURNAL COMPLETED

05:00
06:00
07:00
08:00
09:00
10:00
11:00
12:00
1:00
2:00
3:00
4:00
5:00
6:00
7:00
8:00
9:00

☐ PRAY FOR TODAY, HIS COVERING AS YOU SLEEP, AND HIS PRESENCE TOMORROW
☐ MOVE UNDONE TO-DO'S TO TOMORROW

WATER:
○ ○ ○ ○
○ ○ ○ ○

GOALS:

HOME:

SELF:

WORK:

TO DO:
☐
☐
☐
☐
☐
☐
☐
☐
☐
☐
☐
☐
☐
☐

LAY DOWN YOUR *Sins*

LIFT UP YOUR *Wins*

Journal
RECORD NUDGES FROM DAILY DEVOTION

The Legacy Leaders like to use a popular process of P.R.A.Y. (pause, rejoice, ask, yield) after their daily Devo. As things come to you trust that it is the Holy Spirit nudging you and then do PROBLEM/WORD/GIFT/CHOICE to tap into God's help.

<u>FREE JOURNALING OF WHATEVER IS ON YOUR MIND AS YOU THINK, LISTEN, OR WHAT WEIGHS ON YOUR MIND:</u>

....

....

....

P (PAUSE)

....

R (REJOICE)

....

A (ASK)

....

Y (YIELD)

....

....

<u>WAS THERE ANYTHING YOU FELT NUDGED TO WORK ON? LET'S TAP INTO THE WORD FOR HELP</u>

PROBLEM (EXAMPLES ARE WORRY, FEAR, DOUBT, INSECURITY, IMPATIENCE)
....

WORD (GO TO THE INTERNET & LOOK UP 'MEMORY VERSES ON YOUR TOPIC & RECORD A FEW HERE)
....
....
....

GIFT (WRITE ABOUT WHAT LIFE WOULD LIKE BE IF YOU FOLLOW THE WORD)
....

CHOICE (YOU HAVE FREE WILL, WRITE OUT HOW YOU PLAN TO FOLLOW THROUGH)
....

MEDITATION *Verse*

(REWRITE YESTERDAY'S PROBLEM-WORD-GIFT-CHOICE MEMORY VERSE HERE

Date: _____

| S | M | T | W | T | F | S |

MEALS:

BREAKFAST

LUNCH

DINNER

LAY DOWN YOUR *Sins*

LIFT UP YOUR *Wins*

PRIORITIES:

- [ ] EXERCISED
- [ ] DEVOTIONS & JOURNAL COMPLETED

05:00

06:00

07:00

08:00

09:00

10:00

11:00

12:00

1:00

2:00

3:00

4:00

5:00

6:00

7:00

8:00

9:00

- [ ] PRAY FOR TODAY, HIS COVERING AS YOU SLEEP, AND HIS PRESENCE TOMORROW
- [ ] MOVE UNDONE TO-DO'S TO TOMORROW

WATER:
○ ○ ○ ○
○ ○ ○ ○

GOALS:

HOME:

SELF:

WORK:

TO DO:
- [ ]
- [ ]
- [ ]
- [ ]
- [ ]
- [ ]
- [ ]
- [ ]
- [ ]
- [ ]
- [ ]
- [ ]
- [ ]
- [ ]

Journal
RECORD NUDGES FROM DAILY DEVOTION

The Legacy Leaders like to use a popular process of P.R.A.Y. (pause, rejoice, ask, yield) after their daily Devo. As things come to you trust that it is the Holy Spirit nudging you and then do PROBLEM/WORD/GIFT/CHOICE to tap into God's help.

FREE JOURNALING OF WHATEVER IS ON YOUR MIND AS YOU THINK, LISTEN, OR WHAT WEIGHS ON YOUR MIND:
....
....
....

P (PAUSE)
....

R (REJOICE)
....

A (ASK)
....

Y (YIELD)
....
....

WAS THERE ANYTHING YOU FELT NUDGED TO WORK ON? LET'S TAP INTO THE WORD FOR HELP

PROBLEM (EXAMPLES ARE WORRY, FEAR, DOUBT, INSECURITY, IMPATIENCE)
....

WORD (GO TO THE INTERNET & LOOK UP 'MEMORY VERSES ON YOUR TOPIC & RECORD A FEW HERE)
....
....
....

GIFT (WRITE ABOUT WHAT LIFE WOULD LIKE BE IF YOU FOLLOW THE WORD)
....

CHOICE (YOU HAVE FREE WILL, WRITE OUT HOW YOU PLAN TO FOLLOW THROUGH)
....
....

MEDITATION *Verse*

(REWRITE YESTERDAY'S PROBLEM-WORD-GIFT-CHOICE MEMORY VERSE HERE

Date: _____
| S | M | T | W | T | F | S |

MEALS:

BREAKFAST

LUNCH

DINNER

PRIORITIES:

- [ ] EXERCISED
- [ ] DEVOTIONS & JOURNAL COMPLETED

05:00
06:00
07:00
08:00
09:00
10:00
11:00
12:00
1:00
2:00
3:00
4:00
5:00
6:00
7:00
8:00
9:00

WATER:
○ ○ ○ ○
○ ○ ○ ○

GOALS:

HOME:

SELF:

WORK:

TO DO:

LAY DOWN YOUR *Sins*

LIFT UP YOUR *Wins*

- [ ] PRAY FOR TODAY, HIS COVERING AS YOU SLEEP, AND HIS PRESENCE TOMORROW
- [ ] MOVE UNDONE TO-DO'S TO TOMORROW

Journal
RECORD NUDGES FROM DAILY DEVOTION

The Legacy Leaders like to use a popular process of P.R.A.Y. (pause, rejoice, ask, yield) after their daily Devo. As things come to you trust that it is the Holy Spirit nudging you and then do PROBLEM/WORD/GIFT/CHOICE to tap into God's help.

FREE JOURNALING OF WHATEVER IS ON YOUR MIND AS YOU THINK, LISTEN, OR WHAT WEIGHS ON YOUR MIND:

....
....
....

P (PAUSE)
....

R (REJOICE)
....

A (ASK)
....

Y (YIELD)
....
....

WAS THERE ANYTHING YOU FELT NUDGED TO WORK ON? LET'S TAP INTO THE WORD FOR HELP

PROBLEM (EXAMPLES ARE WORRY, FEAR, DOUBT, INSECURITY, IMPATIENCE)
....

WORD (GO TO THE INTERNET & LOOK UP 'MEMORY VERSES ON YOUR TOPIC & RECORD A FEW HERE)
....
....
....

GIFT (WRITE ABOUT WHAT LIFE WOULD LIKE BE IF YOU FOLLOW THE WORD)
....

CHOICE (YOU HAVE FREE WILL, WRITE OUT HOW YOU PLAN TO FOLLOW THROUGH)
....
....

MEDITATION *Verse*

(REWRITE YESTERDAY'S PROBLEM-WORD-GIFT-CHOICE MEMORY VERSE HERE)

Date: _____

| S | M | T | W | T | F | S |

MEALS:

BREAKFAST

LUNCH

DINNER

PRIORITIES:

☐ EXERCISED
☐ DEVOTIONS & JOURNAL COMPLETED

- 05:00
- 06:00
- 07:00
- 08:00
- 09:00
- 10:00
- 11:00
- 12:00
- 1:00
- 2:00
- 3:00
- 4:00
- 5:00
- 6:00
- 7:00
- 8:00
- 9:00

WATER:
○ ○ ○ ○
○ ○ ○ ○

GOALS:

HOME:

SELF:

WORK:

TO DO:
☐
☐
☐
☐
☐
☐
☐
☐
☐
☐
☐
☐
☐

LAY DOWN YOUR *Sins*

LIFT UP YOUR *Wins*

☐ PRAY FOR TODAY, HIS COVERING AS YOU SLEEP, AND HIS PRESENCE TOMORROW
☐ MOVE UNDONE TO-DO'S TO TOMORROW

Journal
RECORD NUDGES FROM DAILY DEVOTION

The Legacy Leaders like to use a popular process of P.R.A.Y. (pause, rejoice, ask, yield) after their daily Devo. As things come to you trust that it is the Holy Spirit nudging you and then do PROBLEM/WORD/GIFT/CHOICE to tap into God's help.

FREE JOURNALING OF WHATEVER IS ON YOUR MIND AS YOU THINK, LISTEN, OR WHAT WEIGHS ON YOUR MIND:

....

....

....

P (PAUSE)
....

R (REJOICE)
....

A (ASK)
....

Y (YIELD)
....

....

WAS THERE ANYTHING YOU FELT NUDGED TO WORK ON? LET'S TAP INTO THE WORD FOR HELP

PROBLEM (EXAMPLES ARE WORRY, FEAR, DOUBT, INSECURITY, IMPATIENCE)
....

WORD (GO TO THE INTERNET & LOOK UP 'MEMORY VERSES ON YOUR TOPIC & RECORD A FEW HERE)
....

....

....

GIFT (WRITE ABOUT WHAT LIFE WOULD LIKE BE IF YOU FOLLOW THE WORD)
....

CHOICE (YOU HAVE FREE WILL, WRITE OUT HOW YOU PLAN TO FOLLOW THROUGH)
....

....

MEDITATION *Verse*

(REWRITE YESTERDAY'S PROBLEM-WORD-GIFT-CHOICE MEMORY VERSE HERE)

Date: _____

| S | M | T | W | T | F | S |

MEALS:

BREAKFAST

LUNCH

DINNER

PRIORITIES:

☐ EXERCISED
☐ DEVOTIONS & JOURNAL COMPLETED

- 05:00
- 06:00
- 07:00
- 08:00
- 09:00
- 10:00
- 11:00
- 12:00
- 1:00
- 2:00
- 3:00
- 4:00
- 5:00
- 6:00
- 7:00
- 8:00
- 9:00

WATER:
○ ○ ○ ○
○ ○ ○ ○

GOALS:

HOME:

SELF:

WORK:

TO DO:
☐
☐
☐
☐
☐
☐
☐
☐
☐
☐
☐
☐

LAY DOWN YOUR *Sins*

LIFT UP YOUR *Wins*

☐ PRAY FOR TODAY, HIS COVERING AS YOU SLEEP, AND HIS PRESENCE TOMORROW
☐ MOVE UNDONE TO-DO'S TO TOMORROW

Journal
RECORD NUDGES FROM DAILY DEVOTION

The Legacy Leaders like to use a popular process of P.R.A.Y. (pause, rejoice, ask, yield) after their daily Devo. As things come to you trust that it is the Holy Spirit nudging you and then do PROBLEM/WORD/GIFT/CHOICE to tap into God's help.

FREE JOURNALING OF WHATEVER IS ON YOUR MIND AS YOU THINK, LISTEN, OR WHAT WEIGHS ON YOUR MIND:

P (PAUSE)

R (REJOICE)

A (ASK)

Y (YIELD)

WAS THERE ANYTHING YOU FELT NUDGED TO WORK ON? LET'S TAP INTO THE WORD FOR HELP

PROBLEM (EXAMPLES ARE WORRY, FEAR, DOUBT, INSECURITY, IMPATIENCE)

WORD (GO TO THE INTERNET & LOOK UP 'MEMORY VERSES ON YOUR TOPIC & RECORD A FEW HERE)

GIFT (WRITE ABOUT WHAT LIFE WOULD LIKE BE IF YOU FOLLOW THE WORD)

CHOICE (YOU HAVE FREE WILL, WRITE OUT HOW YOU PLAN TO FOLLOW THROUGH)

MEDITATION *Verse*

(REWRITE YESTERDAY'S PROBLEM-WORD-GIFT-CHOICE MEMORY VERSE HERE)

Date: _____

| S | M | T | W | T | F | S |

MEALS:

BREAKFAST

LUNCH

DINNER

PRIORITIES:

- [ ] EXERCISED
- [ ] DEVOTIONS & JOURNAL COMPLETED

05:00
06:00
07:00
08:00
09:00
10:00
11:00
12:00
1:00
2:00
3:00
4:00
5:00
6:00
7:00
8:00
9:00

WATER:
○ ○ ○ ○
○ ○ ○ ○

GOALS:

HOME:

SELF:

WORK:

TO DO:
- [ ]
- [ ]
- [ ]
- [ ]
- [ ]
- [ ]
- [ ]
- [ ]
- [ ]
- [ ]
- [ ]
- [ ]
- [ ]
- [ ]
- [ ]
- [ ]
- [ ]

LAY DOWN YOUR *Sins*

LIFT UP YOUR *Wins*

- [ ] PRAY FOR TODAY, HIS COVERING AS YOU SLEEP, AND HIS PRESENCE TOMORROW
- [ ] MOVE UNDONE TO-DO'S TO TOMORROW

Journal
RECORD NUDGES FROM DAILY DEVOTION

The Legacy Leaders like to use a popular process of P.R.A.Y. (pause, rejoice, ask, yield) after their daily Devo. As things come to you trust that it is the Holy Spirit nudging you and then do PROBLEM/WORD/GIFT/CHOICE to tap into God's help.

FREE JOURNALING OF WHATEVER IS ON YOUR MIND AS YOU THINK, LISTEN, OR WHAT WEIGHS ON YOUR MIND:

....
....
....

P (PAUSE)
....

R (REJOICE)
....

A (ASK)
....

Y (YIELD)
....
....

WAS THERE ANYTHING YOU FELT NUDGED TO WORK ON? LET'S TAP INTO THE WORD FOR HELP

PROBLEM (EXAMPLES ARE WORRY, FEAR, DOUBT, INSECURITY, IMPATIENCE)
....

WORD (GO TO THE INTERNET & LOOK UP 'MEMORY VERSES ON YOUR TOPIC & RECORD A FEW HERE)
....
....
....

GIFT (WRITE ABOUT WHAT LIFE WOULD LIKE BE IF YOU FOLLOW THE WORD)
....

CHOICE (YOU HAVE FREE WILL, WRITE OUT HOW YOU PLAN TO FOLLOW THROUGH)
....
....

MEDITATION *Verse*

(REWRITE YESTERDAY'S PROBLEM-WORD-GIFT-CHOICE MEMORY VERSE HERE

Date: _____

| S | M | T | W | T | F | S |

MEALS:

BREAKFAST

LUNCH

DINNER

PRIORITIES:

- [ ] EXERCISED
- [ ] DEVOTIONS & JOURNAL COMPLETED

- 05:00
- 06:00
- 07:00
- 08:00
- 09:00
- 10:00
- 11:00
- 12:00
- 1:00
- 2:00
- 3:00
- 4:00
- 5:00
- 6:00
- 7:00
- 8:00
- 9:00

WATER:
○ ○ ○ ○
○ ○ ○ ○

GOALS:

HOME:

SELF:

WORK:

TO DO:
- [ ]
- [ ]
- [ ]
- [ ]
- [ ]
- [ ]
- [ ]
- [ ]
- [ ]
- [ ]
- [ ]
- [ ]
- [ ]
- [ ]
- [ ]
- [ ]
- [ ]

LAY DOWN YOUR *Sins*

LIFT UP YOUR *Wins*

- [ ] PRAY FOR TODAY, HIS COVERING AS YOU SLEEP, AND HIS PRESENCE TOMORROW
- [ ] MOVE UNDONE TO-DO'S TO TOMORROW

Journal
RECORD NUDGES FROM DAILY DEVOTION

The Legacy Leaders like to use a popular process of P.R.A.Y. (pause, rejoice, ask, yield) after their daily Devo. As things come to you trust that it is the Holy Spirit nudging you and then do PROBLEM/WORD/GIFT/CHOICE to tap into God's help.

FREE JOURNALING OF WHATEVER IS ON YOUR MIND AS YOU THINK, LISTEN, OR WHAT WEIGHS ON YOUR MIND:

....
....
....
....

P (PAUSE)
....

R (REJOICE)
....

A (ASK)
....

Y (YIELD)
....
....

WAS THERE ANYTHING YOU FELT NUDGED TO WORK ON? LET'S TAP INTO THE WORD FOR HELP

PROBLEM (EXAMPLES ARE WORRY, FEAR, DOUBT, INSECURITY, IMPATIENCE)
....

WORD (GO TO THE INTERNET & LOOK UP 'MEMORY VERSES ON YOUR TOPIC & RECORD A FEW HERE)
....
....
....

GIFT (WRITE ABOUT WHAT LIFE WOULD LIKE BE IF YOU FOLLOW THE WORD)
....

CHOICE (YOU HAVE FREE WILL, WRITE OUT HOW YOU PLAN TO FOLLOW THROUGH)
....

MEDITATION *Verse*

(REWRITE YESTERDAY'S PROBLEM-WORD-GIFT-CHOICE MEMORY VERSE HERE)

Date: _____

| S | M | T | W | T | F | S |

MEALS:

BREAKFAST

LUNCH

DINNER

PRIORITIES:

☐ EXERCISED
☐ DEVOTIONS & JOURNAL COMPLETED

- 05:00
- 06:00
- 07:00
- 08:00
- 09:00
- 10:00
- 11:00
- 12:00
- 1:00
- 2:00
- 3:00
- 4:00
- 5:00
- 6:00
- 7:00
- 8:00
- 9:00

WATER:
○ ○ ○ ○
○ ○ ○ ○

GOALS:

HOME:

SELF:

WORK:

TO DO:
☐
☐
☐
☐
☐
☐
☐
☐
☐
☐
☐
☐
☐
☐
☐

LAY DOWN YOUR *Sins*

LIFT UP YOUR *Wins*

☐ PRAY FOR TODAY, HIS COVERING AS YOU SLEEP, AND HIS PRESENCE TOMORROW
☐ MOVE UNDONE TO-DO'S TO TOMORROW

Journal
RECORD NUDGES FROM DAILY DEVOTION

The Legacy Leaders like to use a popular process of P.R.A.Y. (pause, rejoice, ask, yield) after their daily Devo. As things come to you trust that it is the Holy Spirit nudging you and then do PROBLEM/WORD/GIFT/CHOICE to tap into God's help.

FREE JOURNALING OF WHATEVER IS ON YOUR MIND AS YOU THINK, LISTEN, OR WHAT WEIGHS ON YOUR MIND:

P (PAUSE)

R (REJOICE)

A (ASK)

Y (YIELD)

WAS THERE ANYTHING YOU FELT NUDGED TO WORK ON? LET'S TAP INTO THE WORD FOR HELP

PROBLEM (EXAMPLES ARE WORRY, FEAR, DOUBT, INSECURITY, IMPATIENCE)

WORD (GO TO THE INTERNET & LOOK UP 'MEMORY VERSES ON YOUR TOPIC & RECORD A FEW HERE)

GIFT (WRITE ABOUT WHAT LIFE WOULD LIKE BE IF YOU FOLLOW THE WORD)

CHOICE (YOU HAVE FREE WILL, WRITE OUT HOW YOU PLAN TO FOLLOW THROUGH)

MEDITATION *Verse*

(REWRITE YESTERDAY'S PROBLEM-WORD-GIFT-CHOICE MEMORY VERSE HERE

Date: _____

| S | M | T | W | T | F | S |

MEALS:

BREAKFAST

LUNCH

DINNER

PRIORITIES:

- [ ] EXERCISED
- [ ] DEVOTIONS & JOURNAL COMPLETED

05:00
06:00
07:00
08:00
09:00
10:00
11:00
12:00
1:00
2:00
3:00
4:00
5:00
6:00
7:00
8:00
9:00

WATER:
○ ○ ○ ○
○ ○ ○ ○

GOALS:

HOME:

SELF:

WORK:

TO DO:
- [ ]
- [ ]
- [ ]
- [ ]
- [ ]
- [ ]
- [ ]
- [ ]
- [ ]
- [ ]
- [ ]
- [ ]
- [ ]
- [ ]
- [ ]
- [ ]

LAY DOWN YOUR *Sins*

LIFT UP YOUR *Wins*

- [ ] PRAY FOR TODAY, HIS COVERING AS YOU SLEEP, AND HIS PRESENCE TOMORROW
- [ ] MOVE UNDONE TO-DO'S TO TOMORROW

Journal
RECORD NUDGES FROM DAILY DEVOTION

The Legacy Leaders like to use a popular process of P.R.A.Y. (pause, rejoice, ask, yield) after their daily Devo. As things come to you trust that it is the Holy Spirit nudging you and then do PROBLEM/WORD/GIFT/CHOICE to tap into God's help.

FREE JOURNALING OF WHATEVER IS ON YOUR MIND AS YOU THINK, LISTEN, OR WHAT WEIGHS ON YOUR MIND:

....

....

....

P (PAUSE)
....

R (REJOICE)
....

A (ASK)
....

Y (YIELD)
....

....

WAS THERE ANYTHING YOU FELT NUDGED TO WORK ON? LET'S TAP INTO THE WORD FOR HELP

PROBLEM (EXAMPLES ARE WORRY, FEAR, DOUBT, INSECURITY, IMPATIENCE)
....

WORD (GO TO THE INTERNET & LOOK UP 'MEMORY VERSES ON YOUR TOPIC & RECORD A FEW HERE)
....

....

....

GIFT (WRITE ABOUT WHAT LIFE WOULD LIKE BE IF YOU FOLLOW THE WORD)
....

CHOICE (YOU HAVE FREE WILL, WRITE OUT HOW YOU PLAN TO FOLLOW THROUGH)
....

....

MEDITATION *Verse*

(REWRITE YESTERDAY'S PROBLEM-WORD-GIFT-CHOICE MEMORY VERSE HERE

Date: _____

| S | M | T | W | T | F | S |

MEALS:

BREAKFAST

LUNCH

DINNER

PRIORITIES:

☐ EXERCISED
☐ DEVOTIONS & JOURNAL COMPLETED

- 05:00
- 06:00
- 07:00
- 08:00
- 09:00
- 10:00
- 11:00
- 12:00
- 1:00
- 2:00
- 3:00
- 4:00
- 5:00
- 6:00
- 7:00
- 8:00
- 9:00

WATER:
○ ○ ○ ○
○ ○ ○ ○

GOALS:

HOME:

SELF:

WORK:

TO DO:
☐
☐
☐
☐
☐
☐
☐
☐
☐
☐
☐
☐
☐
☐
☐

LAY DOWN YOUR *Sins*

LIFT UP YOUR *Wins*

☐ PRAY FOR TODAY, HIS COVERING AS YOU SLEEP, AND HIS PRESENCE TOMORROW
☐ MOVE UNDONE TO-DO'S TO TOMORROW

Journal
RECORD NUDGES FROM DAILY DEVOTION

The Legacy Leaders like to use a popular process of P.R.A.Y. (pause, rejoice, ask, yield) after their daily Devo. As things come to you trust that it is the Holy Spirit nudging you and then do PROBLEM/WORD/GIFT/CHOICE to tap into God's help.

FREE JOURNALING OF WHATEVER IS ON YOUR MIND AS YOU THINK, LISTEN, OR WHAT WEIGHS ON YOUR MIND:

P (PAUSE)

R (REJOICE)

A (ASK)

Y (YIELD)

WAS THERE ANYTHING YOU FELT NUDGED TO WORK ON? LET'S TAP INTO THE WORD FOR HELP

PROBLEM (EXAMPLES ARE WORRY, FEAR, DOUBT, INSECURITY, IMPATIENCE)

WORD (GO TO THE INTERNET & LOOK UP 'MEMORY VERSES ON YOUR TOPIC & RECORD A FEW HERE)

GIFT (WRITE ABOUT WHAT LIFE WOULD LIKE BE IF YOU FOLLOW THE WORD)

CHOICE (YOU HAVE FREE WILL. WRITE OUT HOW YOU PLAN TO FOLLOW THROUGH)

MEDITATION *Verse*

(REWRITE YESTERDAY'S PROBLEM-WORD-GIFT-CHOICE MEMORY VERSE HERE)

Date: _____

| S | M | T | W | T | F | S |

MEALS:

BREAKFAST

LUNCH

DINNER

PRIORITIES:

☐ EXERCISED
☐ DEVOTIONS & JOURNAL COMPLETED

- 05:00
- 06:00
- 07:00
- 08:00
- 09:00
- 10:00
- 11:00
- 12:00
- 1:00
- 2:00
- 3:00
- 4:00
- 5:00
- 6:00
- 7:00
- 8:00
- 9:00

WATER:
○ ○ ○ ○
○ ○ ○ ○

GOALS:

HOME:

SELF:

WORK:

TO DO:
☐
☐
☐
☐
☐
☐
☐
☐
☐
☐
☐
☐
☐
☐

LAY DOWN YOUR *Sins*

LIFT UP YOUR *Wins*

☐ PRAY FOR TODAY, HIS COVERING AS YOU SLEEP, AND HIS PRESENCE TOMORROW
☐ MOVE UNDONE TO-DO'S TO TOMORROW

Journal
RECORD NUDGES FROM DAILY DEVOTION

The Legacy Leaders like to use a popular process of P.R.A.Y. (pause, rejoice, ask, yield) after their daily Devo. As things come to you trust that it is the Holy Spirit nudging you and then do PROBLEM/WORD/GIFT/CHOICE to tap into God's help.

FREE JOURNALING OF WHATEVER IS ON YOUR MIND AS YOU THINK, LISTEN, OR WHAT WEIGHS ON YOUR MIND:

....
....
....

P (PAUSE)
....

R (REJOICE)
....

A (ASK)
....

Y (YIELD)
....
....

WAS THERE ANYTHING YOU FELT NUDGED TO WORK ON? LET'S TAP INTO THE WORD FOR HELP

PROBLEM (EXAMPLES ARE WORRY, FEAR, DOUBT, INSECURITY, IMPATIENCE)
....

WORD (GO TO THE INTERNET & LOOK UP 'MEMORY VERSES ON YOUR TOPIC & RECORD A FEW HERE)
....
....
....

GIFT (WRITE ABOUT WHAT LIFE WOULD LIKE BE IF YOU FOLLOW THE WORD)
....

CHOICE (YOU HAVE FREE WILL, WRITE OUT HOW YOU PLAN TO FOLLOW THROUGH)
....

MEDITATION *Verse*

(REWRITE YESTERDAY'S PROBLEM-WORD-GIFT-CHOICE MEMORY VERSE HERE)

Date: _____

| S | M | T | W | T | F | S |

MEALS:

BREAKFAST

LUNCH

DINNER

PRIORITIES:

- [ ] EXERCISED
- [ ] DEVOTIONS & JOURNAL COMPLETED

05:00
06:00
07:00
08:00
09:00
10:00
11:00
12:00
1:00
2:00
3:00
4:00
5:00
6:00
7:00
8:00
9:00

- [ ] PRAY FOR TODAY, HIS COVERING AS YOU SLEEP, AND HIS PRESENCE TOMORROW
- [ ] MOVE UNDONE TO-DO'S TO TOMORROW

WATER:
○ ○ ○ ○
○ ○ ○ ○

GOALS:

HOME:

SELF:

WORK:

TO DO:
- [ ]
- [ ]
- [ ]
- [ ]
- [ ]
- [ ]
- [ ]
- [ ]
- [ ]
- [ ]
- [ ]
- [ ]
- [ ]
- [ ]
- [ ]
- [ ]

LAY DOWN YOUR *Sins*

LIFT UP YOUR *Wins*

Journal
RECORD NUDGES FROM DAILY DEVOTION

The Legacy Leaders like to use a popular process of P.R.A.Y. (pause, rejoice, ask, yield) after their daily Devo. As things come to you trust that it is the Holy Spirit nudging you and then do PROBLEM/WORD/GIFT/CHOICE to tap into God's help.

FREE JOURNALING OF WHATEVER IS ON YOUR MIND AS YOU THINK, LISTEN, OR WHAT WEIGHS ON YOUR MIND:

....
....
....

P (PAUSE)
....

R (REJOICE)
....

A (ASK)
....

Y (YIELD)
....

WAS THERE ANYTHING YOU FELT NUDGED TO WORK ON? LET'S TAP INTO THE WORD FOR HELP

PROBLEM (EXAMPLES ARE WORRY, FEAR, DOUBT, INSECURITY, IMPATIENCE)
....

WORD (GO TO THE INTERNET & LOOK UP 'MEMORY VERSES ON YOUR TOPIC & RECORD A FEW HERE)
....
....
....

GIFT (WRITE ABOUT WHAT LIFE WOULD LIKE BE IF YOU FOLLOW THE WORD)
....

CHOICE (YOU HAVE FREE WILL, WRITE OUT HOW YOU PLAN TO FOLLOW THROUGH)
....

MEDITATION *Verse*

(REWRITE YESTERDAY'S PROBLEM-WORD-GIFT-CHOICE MEMORY VERSE HERE

Date: _____

| S | M | T | W | T | F | S |

MEALS:

BREAKFAST

LUNCH

DINNER

PRIORITIES:

- [ ] EXERCISED
- [ ] DEVOTIONS & JOURNAL COMPLETED

05:00
06:00
07:00
08:00
09:00
10:00
11:00
12:00
1:00
2:00
3:00
4:00
5:00
6:00
7:00
8:00
9:00

- [ ] PRAY FOR TODAY, HIS COVERING AS YOU SLEEP, AND HIS PRESENCE TOMORROW
- [ ] MOVE UNDONE TO-DO'S TO TOMORROW

WATER:
○ ○ ○ ○
○ ○ ○ ○

GOALS:

HOME:

SELF:

WORK:

TO DO:
- [ ]
- [ ]
- [ ]
- [ ]
- [ ]
- [ ]
- [ ]
- [ ]
- [ ]
- [ ]
- [ ]
- [ ]
- [ ]
- [ ]
- [ ]
- [ ]
- [ ]

LAY DOWN YOUR *Sins*

LIFT UP YOUR *Wins*

Journal
RECORD NUDGES FROM DAILY DEVOTION

The Legacy Leaders like to use a popular process of P.R.A.Y. (pause, rejoice, ask, yield) after their daily Devo. As things come to you trust that it is the Holy Spirit nudging you and then do PROBLEM/WORD/GIFT/CHOICE to tap into God's help.

FREE JOURNALING OF WHATEVER IS ON YOUR MIND AS YOU THINK, LISTEN, OR WHAT WEIGHS ON YOUR MIND:

....
....
....

P (PAUSE)
....

R (REJOICE)
....

A (ASK)
....

Y (YIELD)
....
....

WAS THERE ANYTHING YOU FELT NUDGED TO WORK ON? LET'S TAP INTO THE WORD FOR HELP

PROBLEM (EXAMPLES ARE WORRY, FEAR, DOUBT, INSECURITY, IMPATIENCE) ....

WORD (GO TO THE INTERNET & LOOK UP 'MEMORY VERSES ON YOUR TOPIC & RECORD A FEW HERE)
....
....

GIFT (WRITE ABOUT WHAT LIFE WOULD LIKE BE IF YOU FOLLOW THE WORD) ....

CHOICE (YOU HAVE FREE WILL. WRITE OUT HOW YOU PLAN TO FOLLOW THROUGH)
....

MEDITATION *Verse*

(REWRITE YESTERDAY'S PROBLEM-WORD-GIFT-CHOICE MEMORY VERSE HERE)

Date: _____

| S | M | T | W | T | F | S |

MEALS:

BREAKFAST

LUNCH

DINNER

PRIORITIES:

☐ EXERCISED
☐ DEVOTIONS & JOURNAL COMPLETED

05:00
06:00
07:00
08:00
09:00
10:00
11:00
12:00
1:00
2:00
3:00
4:00
5:00
6:00
7:00
8:00
9:00

WATER:
○ ○ ○ ○
○ ○ ○ ○

GOALS:

HOME:

SELF:

WORK:

TO DO:
☐
☐
☐
☐
☐
☐
☐
☐
☐
☐
☐
☐
☐
☐
☐

LAY DOWN YOUR *Sins*

LIFT UP YOUR *Wins*

☐ PRAY FOR TODAY, HIS COVERING AS YOU SLEEP, AND HIS PRESENCE TOMORROW
☐ MOVE UNDONE TO-DO'S TO TOMORROW

Journal
RECORD NUDGES FROM DAILY DEVOTION

The Legacy Leaders like to use a popular process of P.R.A.Y. (pause, rejoice, ask, yield) after their daily Devo. As things come to you trust that it is the Holy Spirit nudging you and then do PROBLEM/WORD/GIFT/CHOICE to tap into God's help.

FREE JOURNALING OF WHATEVER IS ON YOUR MIND AS YOU THINK, LISTEN, OR WHAT WEIGHS ON YOUR MIND:

P (PAUSE)

R (REJOICE)

A (ASK)

Y (YIELD)

WAS THERE ANYTHING YOU FELT NUDGED TO WORK ON? LET'S TAP INTO THE WORD FOR HELP

PROBLEM (EXAMPLES ARE WORRY, FEAR, DOUBT, INSECURITY, IMPATIENCE)

WORD (GO TO THE INTERNET & LOOK UP 'MEMORY VERSES ON YOUR TOPIC & RECORD A FEW HERE)

GIFT (WRITE ABOUT WHAT LIFE WOULD LIKE BE IF YOU FOLLOW THE WORD)

CHOICE (YOU HAVE FREE WILL, WRITE OUT HOW YOU PLAN TO FOLLOW THROUGH)

MEDITATION *Verse*

(REWRITE YESTERDAY'S PROBLEM-WORD-GIFT-CHOICE MEMORY VERSE HERE)

Date: _____

| S | M | T | W | T | F | S |

MEALS:

BREAKFAST

LUNCH

DINNER

PRIORITIES:

- [ ] EXERCISED
- [ ] DEVOTIONS & JOURNAL COMPLETED

05:00
06:00
07:00
08:00
09:00
10:00
11:00
12:00
1:00
2:00
3:00
4:00
5:00
6:00
7:00
8:00
9:00

WATER:
○ ○ ○ ○
○ ○ ○ ○

GOALS:

HOME:

SELF:

WORK:

TO DO:
- [ ]
- [ ]
- [ ]
- [ ]
- [ ]
- [ ]
- [ ]
- [ ]
- [ ]
- [ ]
- [ ]
- [ ]
- [ ]
- [ ]
- [ ]

LAY DOWN YOUR *Sins*

LIFT UP YOUR *Wins*

- [ ] PRAY FOR TODAY, HIS COVERING AS YOU SLEEP, AND HIS PRESENCE TOMORROW
- [ ] MOVE UNDONE TO-DO'S TO TOMORROW

Journal
RECORD NUDGES FROM DAILY DEVOTION

The Legacy Leaders like to use a popular process of P.R.A.Y. (pause, rejoice, ask, yield) after their daily Devo. As things come to you trust that it is the Holy Spirit nudging you and then do PROBLEM/WORD/GIFT/CHOICE to tap into God's help.

FREE JOURNALING OF WHATEVER IS ON YOUR MIND AS YOU THINK, LISTEN, OR WHAT WEIGHS ON YOUR MIND:

P (PAUSE)

R (REJOICE)

A (ASK)

Y (YIELD)

WAS THERE ANYTHING YOU FELT NUDGED TO WORK ON? LET'S TAP INTO THE WORD FOR HELP

PROBLEM (EXAMPLES ARE WORRY, FEAR, DOUBT, INSECURITY, IMPATIENCE)

WORD (GO TO THE INTERNET & LOOK UP 'MEMORY VERSES ON YOUR TOPIC & RECORD A FEW HERE)

GIFT (WRITE ABOUT WHAT LIFE WOULD LIKE BE IF YOU FOLLOW THE WORD)

CHOICE (YOU HAVE FREE WILL, WRITE OUT HOW YOU PLAN TO FOLLOW THROUGH)

MEDITATION *Verse*

(REWRITE YESTERDAY'S PROBLEM-WORD-GIFT-CHOICE MEMORY VERSE HERE)

Date: _____

| S | M | T | W | T | F | S |

MEALS:

BREAKFAST

LUNCH

DINNER

PRIORITIES:

- [ ] EXERCISED
- [ ] DEVOTIONS & JOURNAL COMPLETED

05:00
06:00
07:00
08:00
09:00
10:00
11:00
12:00
1:00
2:00
3:00
4:00
5:00
6:00
7:00
8:00
9:00

WATER:
○ ○ ○ ○
○ ○ ○ ○

GOALS:

HOME:

SELF:

WORK:

TO DO:
- [ ]
- [ ]
- [ ]
- [ ]
- [ ]
- [ ]
- [ ]
- [ ]
- [ ]
- [ ]
- [ ]
- [ ]
- [ ]
- [ ]
- [ ]
- [ ]
- [ ]

LAY DOWN YOUR *Sins*

LIFT UP YOUR *Wins*

- [ ] PRAY FOR TODAY, HIS COVERING AS YOU SLEEP, AND HIS PRESENCE TOMORROW
- [ ] MOVE UNDONE TO-DO'S TO TOMORROW

Journal
RECORD NUDGES FROM DAILY DEVOTION

The Legacy Leaders like to use a popular process of P.R.A.Y. (pause, rejoice, ask, yield) after their daily Devo. As things come to you trust that it is the Holy Spirit nudging you and then do PROBLEM/WORD/GIFT/CHOICE to tap into God's help.

<u>FREE JOURNALING OF WHATEVER IS ON YOUR MIND AS YOU THINK, LISTEN, OR WHAT WEIGHS ON YOUR MIND:</u>

P (PAUSE)

R (REJOICE)

A (ASK)

Y (YIELD)

<u>WAS THERE ANYTHING YOU FELT NUDGED TO WORK ON? LET'S TAP INTO THE WORD FOR HELP</u>

PROBLEM (EXAMPLES ARE WORRY, FEAR, DOUBT, INSECURITY, IMPATIENCE)

WORD (GO TO THE INTERNET & LOOK UP 'MEMORY VERSES ON YOUR TOPIC & RECORD A FEW HERE)

GIFT (WRITE ABOUT WHAT LIFE WOULD LIKE BE IF YOU FOLLOW THE WORD)

CHOICE (YOU HAVE FREE WILL, WRITE OUT HOW YOU PLAN TO FOLLOW THROUGH)

MEDITATION *Verse*

(REWRITE YESTERDAY'S PROBLEM-WORD-GIFT-CHOICE MEMORY VERSE HERE

Date: _____

| S | M | T | W | T | F | S |

MEALS:

BREAKFAST

LUNCH

DINNER

PRIORITIES:

☐ EXERCISED
☐ DEVOTIONS & JOURNAL COMPLETED

05:00
06:00
07:00
08:00
09:00
10:00
11:00
12:00
1:00
2:00
3:00
4:00
5:00
6:00
7:00
8:00
9:00

WATER:
○ ○ ○ ○
○ ○ ○ ○

GOALS:

HOME:

SELF:

WORK:

TO DO:
☐
☐
☐
☐
☐
☐
☐
☐
☐
☐
☐
☐
☐
☐
☐

LAY DOWN YOUR *Sins*

LIFT UP YOUR *Wins*

☐ PRAY FOR TODAY, HIS COVERING AS YOU SLEEP, AND HIS PRESENCE TOMORROW
☐ MOVE UNDONE TO-DO'S TO TOMORROW

Journal
RECORD NUDGES FROM DAILY DEVOTION

The Legacy Leaders like to use a popular process of P.R.A.Y. (pause, rejoice, ask, yield) after their daily Devo. As things come to you trust that it is the Holy Spirit nudging you and then do PROBLEM/WORD/GIFT/CHOICE to tap into God's help.

FREE JOURNALING OF WHATEVER IS ON YOUR MIND AS YOU THINK, LISTEN, OR WHAT WEIGHS ON YOUR MIND:

....
....
....

P (PAUSE)
....

R (REJOICE)
....

A (ASK)
....

Y (YIELD)
....
....

WAS THERE ANYTHING YOU FELT NUDGED TO WORK ON? LET'S TAP INTO THE WORD FOR HELP

PROBLEM (EXAMPLES ARE WORRY, FEAR, DOUBT, INSECURITY, IMPATIENCE)
....

WORD (GO TO THE INTERNET & LOOK UP 'MEMORY VERSES ON YOUR TOPIC & RECORD A FEW HERE)
....
....
....

GIFT (WRITE ABOUT WHAT LIFE WOULD LIKE BE IF YOU FOLLOW THE WORD)
....

CHOICE (YOU HAVE FREE WILL, WRITE OUT HOW YOU PLAN TO FOLLOW THROUGH)
....

MEDITATION *Verse*

(REWRITE YESTERDAY'S PROBLEM-WORD-GIFT-CHOICE MEMORY VERSE HERE)

Date: _____

| S | M | T | W | T | F | S |

MEALS:

BREAKFAST

LUNCH

DINNER

PRIORITIES:

- [ ] EXERCISED
- [ ] DEVOTIONS & JOURNAL COMPLETED

05:00
06:00
07:00
08:00
09:00
10:00
11:00
12:00
1:00
2:00
3:00
4:00
5:00
6:00
7:00
8:00
9:00

- [ ] PRAY FOR TODAY, HIS COVERING AS YOU SLEEP, AND HIS PRESENCE TOMORROW
- [ ] MOVE UNDONE TO-DO'S TO TOMORROW

WATER:
○ ○ ○ ○
○ ○ ○ ○

GOALS:

HOME:

SELF:

WORK:

TO DO:
- [ ]
- [ ]
- [ ]
- [ ]
- [ ]
- [ ]
- [ ]
- [ ]
- [ ]
- [ ]
- [ ]
- [ ]
- [ ]
- [ ]
- [ ]
- [ ]
- [ ]

LAY DOWN YOUR *Sins*

LIFT UP YOUR *Wins*

Journal
RECORD NUDGES FROM DAILY DEVOTION

The Legacy Leaders like to use a popular process of P.R.A.Y. (pause, rejoice, ask, yield) after their daily Devo. As things come to you trust that it is the Holy Spirit nudging you and then do PROBLEM/WORD/GIFT/CHOICE to tap into God's help.

FREE JOURNALING OF WHATEVER IS ON YOUR MIND AS YOU THINK, LISTEN, OR WHAT WEIGHS ON YOUR MIND:

....
....
....

P (PAUSE)
....

R (REJOICE)
....

A (ASK)
....

Y (YIELD)
....
....

WAS THERE ANYTHING YOU FELT NUDGED TO WORK ON? LET'S TAP INTO THE WORD FOR HELP

PROBLEM (EXAMPLES ARE WORRY, FEAR, DOUBT, INSECURITY, IMPATIENCE)
....

WORD (GO TO THE INTERNET & LOOK UP 'MEMORY VERSES ON YOUR TOPIC & RECORD A FEW HERE)
....
....
....

GIFT (WRITE ABOUT WHAT LIFE WOULD LIKE BE IF YOU FOLLOW THE WORD)
....

CHOICE (YOU HAVE FREE WILL, WRITE OUT HOW YOU PLAN TO FOLLOW THROUGH)
....
....

MEDITATION *Verse*

(REWRITE YESTERDAY'S PROBLEM-WORD-GIFT-CHOICE MEMORY VERSE HERE)

Date: _____

| S | M | T | W | T | F | S |

MEALS:

BREAKFAST

LUNCH

DINNER

PRIORITIES:

- [ ] EXERCISED
- [ ] DEVOTIONS & JOURNAL COMPLETED

05:00
06:00
07:00
08:00
09:00
10:00
11:00
12:00
1:00
2:00
3:00
4:00
5:00
6:00
7:00
8:00
9:00

WATER:
○ ○ ○ ○
○ ○ ○ ○

GOALS:

HOME:

SELF:

WORK:

TO DO:
- [ ]
- [ ]
- [ ]
- [ ]
- [ ]
- [ ]
- [ ]
- [ ]
- [ ]
- [ ]
- [ ]
- [ ]
- [ ]
- [ ]

LAY DOWN YOUR *Sins*

LIFT UP YOUR *Wins*

- [ ] PRAY FOR TODAY, HIS COVERING AS YOU SLEEP, AND HIS PRESENCE TOMORROW
- [ ] MOVE UNDONE TO-DO'S TO TOMORROW

Journal
RECORD NUDGES FROM DAILY DEVOTION

The Legacy Leaders like to use a popular process of P.R.A.Y. (pause, rejoice, ask, yield) after their daily Devo. As things come to you trust that it is the Holy Spirit nudging you and then do PROBLEM/WORD/GIFT/CHOICE to tap into God's help.

FREE JOURNALING OF WHATEVER IS ON YOUR MIND AS YOU THINK, LISTEN, OR WHAT WEIGHS ON YOUR MIND:

....
....
....

P (PAUSE)
....

R (REJOICE)
....

A (ASK)
....

Y (YIELD)
....

WAS THERE ANYTHING YOU FELT NUDGED TO WORK ON? LET'S TAP INTO THE WORD FOR HELP

PROBLEM (EXAMPLES ARE WORRY, FEAR, DOUBT, INSECURITY, IMPATIENCE)
....

WORD (GO TO THE INTERNET & LOOK UP 'MEMORY VERSES ON YOUR TOPIC & RECORD A FEW HERE)
....
....

GIFT (WRITE ABOUT WHAT LIFE WOULD LIKE BE IF YOU FOLLOW THE WORD)
....

CHOICE (YOU HAVE FREE WILL, WRITE OUT HOW YOU PLAN TO FOLLOW THROUGH)
....

MEDITATION *Verse*

Date: _____

S M T W T F S

(REWRITE YESTERDAY'S PROBLEM-WORD-GIFT-CHOICE MEMORY VERSE HERE)

MEALS:

BREAKFAST

LUNCH

DINNER

PRIORITIES:

- [ ] EXERCISED
- [ ] DEVOTIONS & JOURNAL COMPLETED

05:00
06:00
07:00
08:00
09:00
10:00
11:00
12:00
1:00
2:00
3:00
4:00
5:00
6:00
7:00
8:00
9:00

- [ ] PRAY FOR TODAY, HIS COVERING AS YOU SLEEP, AND HIS PRESENCE TOMORROW
- [ ] MOVE UNDONE TO-DO'S TO TOMORROW

WATER:
○ ○ ○ ○
○ ○ ○ ○

GOALS:

HOME:

SELF:

WORK:

TO DO:
- [ ]
- [ ]
- [ ]
- [ ]
- [ ]
- [ ]
- [ ]
- [ ]
- [ ]
- [ ]
- [ ]
- [ ]
- [ ]
- [ ]
- [ ]
- [ ]
- [ ]
- [ ]

LAY DOWN YOUR *Sins*

LIFT UP YOUR *Wins*

Journal
RECORD NUDGES FROM DAILY DEVOTION

The Legacy Leaders like to use a popular process of P.R.A.Y. (pause, rejoice, ask, yield) after their daily Devo. As things come to you trust that it is the Holy Spirit nudging you and then do PROBLEM/WORD/GIFT/CHOICE to tap into God's help.

FREE JOURNALING OF WHATEVER IS ON YOUR MIND AS YOU THINK, LISTEN, OR WHAT WEIGHS ON YOUR MIND:

_____

_____

_____

P (PAUSE)
_____

R (REJOICE)
_____

A (ASK)
_____

Y (YIELD)
_____

_____

WAS THERE ANYTHING YOU FELT NUDGED TO WORK ON? LET'S TAP INTO THE WORD FOR HELP

PROBLEM (EXAMPLES ARE WORRY, FEAR, DOUBT, INSECURITY, IMPATIENCE)
_____

WORD (GO TO THE INTERNET & LOOK UP 'MEMORY VERSES ON YOUR TOPIC & RECORD A FEW HERE)
_____

_____

GIFT (WRITE ABOUT WHAT LIFE WOULD LIKE BE IF YOU FOLLOW THE WORD)
_____

CHOICE (YOU HAVE FREE WILL, WRITE OUT HOW YOU PLAN TO FOLLOW THROUGH)
_____

MEDITATION *Verse*

(REWRITE YESTERDAY'S PROBLEM-WORD-GIFT-CHOICE MEMORY VERSE HERE)

Date: _____

| S | M | T | W | T | F | S |

MEALS:

BREAKFAST

LUNCH

DINNER

PRIORITIES:

☐ EXERCISED
☐ DEVOTIONS & JOURNAL COMPLETED

05:00
06:00
07:00
08:00
09:00
10:00
11:00
12:00
1:00
2:00
3:00
4:00
5:00
6:00
7:00
8:00
9:00

☐ PRAY FOR TODAY, HIS COVERING AS YOU SLEEP, AND HIS PRESENCE TOMORROW
☐ MOVE UNDONE TO-DO'S TO TOMORROW

WATER:
○ ○ ○
○ ○ ○

GOALS:

HOME:

SELF:

WORK:

TO DO:
☐
☐
☐
☐
☐
☐
☐
☐
☐
☐
☐
☐
☐

LAY DOWN YOUR *Sins*

LIFT UP YOUR *Wins*

Journal
RECORD NUDGES FROM DAILY DEVOTION

The Legacy Leaders like to use a popular process of P.R.A.Y. (pause, rejoice, ask, yield) after their daily Devo. As things come to you trust that it is the Holy Spirit nudging you and then do PROBLEM/WORD/GIFT/CHOICE to tap into God's help.

FREE JOURNALING OF WHATEVER IS ON YOUR MIND AS YOU THINK, LISTEN, OR WHAT WEIGHS ON YOUR MIND:

....

....

....

P (PAUSE)
....

R (REJOICE)
....

A (ASK)
....

Y (YIELD)
....

....

WAS THERE ANYTHING YOU FELT NUDGED TO WORK ON? LET'S TAP INTO THE WORD FOR HELP

PROBLEM (EXAMPLES ARE WORRY, FEAR, DOUBT, INSECURITY, IMPATIENCE)
....

WORD (GO TO THE INTERNET & LOOK UP 'MEMORY VERSES ON YOUR TOPIC & RECORD A FEW HERE)
....

....

GIFT (WRITE ABOUT WHAT LIFE WOULD LIKE BE IF YOU FOLLOW THE WORD)
....

CHOICE (YOU HAVE FREE WILL, WRITE OUT HOW YOU PLAN TO FOLLOW THROUGH)
....

....

MEDITATION *Verse*

(REWRITE YESTERDAY'S PROBLEM-WORD-GIFT-CHOICE MEMORY VERSE HERE)

Date: _____

| S | M | T | W | T | F | S |

MEALS:

BREAKFAST

LUNCH

DINNER

PRIORITIES:
- [ ] EXERCISED
- [ ] DEVOTIONS & JOURNAL COMPLETED

05:00
06:00
07:00
08:00
09:00
10:00
11:00
12:00
1:00
2:00
3:00
4:00
5:00
6:00
7:00
8:00
9:00

WATER:
○ ○ ○ ○
○ ○ ○ ○

GOALS:

HOME:

SELF:

WORK:

TO DO:
- [ ]
- [ ]
- [ ]
- [ ]
- [ ]
- [ ]
- [ ]
- [ ]
- [ ]
- [ ]
- [ ]
- [ ]
- [ ]
- [ ]
- [ ]
- [ ]

LAY DOWN YOUR *Sins*

LIFT UP YOUR *Wins*

- [ ] PRAY FOR TODAY, HIS COVERING AS YOU SLEEP, AND HIS PRESENCE TOMORROW
- [ ] MOVE UNDONE TO-DO'S TO TOMORROW

Journal
RECORD NUDGES FROM DAILY DEVOTION

The Legacy Leaders like to use a popular process of P.R.A.Y. (pause, rejoice, ask, yield) after their daily Devo. As things come to you trust that it is the Holy Spirit nudging you and then do PROBLEM/WORD/GIFT/CHOICE to tap into God's help.

FREE JOURNALING OF WHATEVER IS ON YOUR MIND AS YOU THINK, LISTEN, OR WHAT WEIGHS ON YOUR MIND:

....
....
....
....

P (PAUSE)
....

R (REJOICE)
....

A (ASK)
....

Y (YIELD)
....
....

WAS THERE ANYTHING YOU FELT NUDGED TO WORK ON? LET'S TAP INTO THE WORD FOR HELP

PROBLEM (EXAMPLES ARE WORRY, FEAR, DOUBT, INSECURITY, IMPATIENCE)
....

WORD (GO TO THE INTERNET & LOOK UP 'MEMORY VERSES ON YOUR TOPIC & RECORD A FEW HERE)
....
....
....

GIFT (WRITE ABOUT WHAT LIFE WOULD LIKE BE IF YOU FOLLOW THE WORD)
....

CHOICE (YOU HAVE FREE WILL, WRITE OUT HOW YOU PLAN TO FOLLOW THROUGH)
....
....

MEDITATION *Verse*

(REWRITE YESTERDAY'S PROBLEM-WORD-GIFT-CHOICE MEMORY VERSE HERE

Date: _____

| S | M | T | W | T | F | S |

MEALS:

BREAKFAST

LUNCH

DINNER

PRIORITIES:
- [ ] EXERCISED
- [ ] DEVOTIONS & JOURNAL COMPLETED

05:00
06:00
07:00
08:00
09:00
10:00
11:00
12:00
1:00
2:00
3:00
4:00
5:00
6:00
7:00
8:00
9:00

WATER:
○ ○ ○
○ ○ ○

GOALS:

HOME:

SELF:

WORK:

TO DO:
- [ ]
- [ ]
- [ ]
- [ ]
- [ ]
- [ ]
- [ ]
- [ ]
- [ ]
- [ ]
- [ ]
- [ ]
- [ ]
- [ ]

LAY DOWN YOUR *Sins*

LIFT UP YOUR *Wins*

- [ ] PRAY FOR TODAY, HIS COVERING AS YOU SLEEP, AND HIS PRESENCE TOMORROW
- [ ] MOVE UNDONE TO-DO'S TO TOMORROW

Journal
RECORD NUDGES FROM DAILY DEVOTION

The Legacy Leaders like to use a popular process of P.R.A.Y. (pause, rejoice, ask, yield) after their daily Devo. As things come to you trust that it is the Holy Spirit nudging you and then do PROBLEM/WORD/GIFT/CHOICE to tap into God's help.

FREE JOURNALING OF WHATEVER IS ON YOUR MIND AS YOU THINK, LISTEN, OR WHAT WEIGHS ON YOUR MIND:

....
....
....

P (PAUSE)
....

R (REJOICE)
....

A (ASK)
....

Y (YIELD)
....
....

WAS THERE ANYTHING YOU FELT NUDGED TO WORK ON? LET'S TAP INTO THE WORD FOR HELP

PROBLEM (EXAMPLES ARE WORRY, FEAR, DOUBT, INSECURITY, IMPATIENCE)
....

WORD (GO TO THE INTERNET & LOOK UP 'MEMORY VERSES ON YOUR TOPIC & RECORD A FEW HERE)
....
....
....

GIFT (WRITE ABOUT WHAT LIFE WOULD LIKE BE IF YOU FOLLOW THE WORD)
....

CHOICE (YOU HAVE FREE WILL, WRITE OUT HOW YOU PLAN TO FOLLOW THROUGH)
....
....

MEDITATION *Verse*

(REWRITE YESTERDAY'S PROBLEM-WORD-GIFT-CHOICE MEMORY VERSE HERE

Date:_____

| S | M | T | W | T | F | S |

MEALS:

BREAKFAST

LUNCH

DINNER

PRIORITIES:

- [ ] EXERCISED
- [ ] DEVOTIONS & JOURNAL COMPLETED

05:00
06:00
07:00
08:00
09:00
10:00
11:00
12:00
1:00
2:00
3:00
4:00
5:00
6:00
7:00
8:00
9:00

WATER:
○ ○ ○ ○
○ ○ ○ ○

GOALS:

HOME:

SELF:

WORK:

TO DO:
- [ ]
- [ ]
- [ ]
- [ ]
- [ ]
- [ ]
- [ ]
- [ ]
- [ ]
- [ ]
- [ ]
- [ ]
- [ ]
- [ ]
- [ ]
- [ ]
- [ ]

LAY DOWN YOUR *Sins*

LIFT UP YOUR *Wins*

- [ ] PRAY FOR TODAY, HIS COVERING AS YOU SLEEP, AND HIS PRESENCE TOMORROW
- [ ] MOVE UNDONE TO-DO'S TO TOMORROW

Journal
RECORD NUDGES FROM DAILY DEVOTION

The Legacy Leaders like to use a popular process of P.R.A.Y. (pause, rejoice, ask, yield) after their daily Devo. As things come to you trust that it is the Holy Spirit nudging you and then do PROBLEM/WORD/GIFT/CHOICE to tap into God's help.

FREE JOURNALING OF WHATEVER IS ON YOUR MIND AS YOU THINK, LISTEN, OR WHAT WEIGHS ON YOUR MIND:

P (PAUSE)

R (REJOICE)

A (ASK)

Y (YIELD)

WAS THERE ANYTHING YOU FELT NUDGED TO WORK ON? LET'S TAP INTO THE WORD FOR HELP

PROBLEM (EXAMPLES ARE WORRY, FEAR, DOUBT, INSECURITY, IMPATIENCE)

WORD (GO TO THE INTERNET & LOOK UP 'MEMORY VERSES ON YOUR TOPIC & RECORD A FEW HERE)

GIFT (WRITE ABOUT WHAT LIFE WOULD LIKE BE IF YOU FOLLOW THE WORD)

CHOICE (YOU HAVE FREE WILL, WRITE OUT HOW YOU PLAN TO FOLLOW THROUGH)

MEDITATION *Verse*

(REWRITE YESTERDAY'S PROBLEM-WORD-GIFT-CHOICE MEMORY VERSE HERE

Date: _____

| S | M | T | W | T | F | S |

MEALS:

BREAKFAST

LUNCH

DINNER

PRIORITIES:
- [ ] EXERCISED
- [ ] DEVOTIONS & JOURNAL COMPLETED

05:00
06:00
07:00
08:00
09:00
10:00
11:00
12:00
1:00
2:00
3:00
4:00
5:00
6:00
7:00
8:00
9:00

WATER:
○ ○ ○ ○
○ ○ ○ ○

GOALS:

HOME:

SELF:

WORK:

TO DO:
- [ ]
- [ ]
- [ ]
- [ ]
- [ ]
- [ ]
- [ ]
- [ ]
- [ ]
- [ ]
- [ ]
- [ ]
- [ ]
- [ ]
- [ ]

LAY DOWN YOUR *Sins*

LIFT UP YOUR *Wins*

- [ ] PRAY FOR TODAY, HIS COVERING AS YOU SLEEP, AND HIS PRESENCE TOMORROW
- [ ] MOVE UNDONE TO-DO'S TO TOMORROW

Journal
RECORD NUDGES FROM DAILY DEVOTION

The Legacy Leaders like to use a popular process of P.R.A.Y. (pause, rejoice, ask, yield) after their daily Devo. As things come to you trust that it is the Holy Spirit nudging you and then do PROBLEM/WORD/GIFT/CHOICE to tap into God's help.

<u>FREE JOURNALING OF WHATEVER IS ON YOUR MIND AS YOU THINK, LISTEN, OR WHAT WEIGHS ON YOUR MIND:</u>

....
....
....

P (PAUSE)
....

R (REJOICE)
....

A (ASK)
....

Y (YIELD)
....
....

<u>WAS THERE ANYTHING YOU FELT NUDGED TO WORK ON? LET'S TAP INTO THE WORD FOR HELP</u>

PROBLEM (EXAMPLES ARE WORRY, FEAR, DOUBT, INSECURITY, IMPATIENCE)
....

WORD (GO TO THE INTERNET & LOOK UP 'MEMORY VERSES ON YOUR TOPIC & RECORD A FEW HERE)
....
....
....

GIFT (WRITE ABOUT WHAT LIFE WOULD LIKE BE IF YOU FOLLOW THE WORD)
....

CHOICE (YOU HAVE FREE WILL, WRITE OUT HOW YOU PLAN TO FOLLOW THROUGH)
....
....

MEDITATION *Verse*

(REWRITE YESTERDAY'S PROBLEM-WORD-GIFT-CHOICE MEMORY VERSE HERE)

Date: _____

| S | M | T | W | T | F | S |

MEALS:

BREAKFAST

LUNCH

DINNER

PRIORITIES:

- [ ] EXERCISED
- [ ] DEVOTIONS & JOURNAL COMPLETED

05:00
06:00
07:00
08:00
09:00
10:00
11:00
12:00
1:00
2:00
3:00
4:00
5:00
6:00
7:00
8:00
9:00

- [ ] PRAY FOR TODAY, HIS COVERING AS YOU SLEEP, AND HIS PRESENCE TOMORROW
- [ ] MOVE UNDONE TO-DO'S TO TOMORROW

WATER:
○ ○ ○
○ ○ ○

GOALS:

HOME:

SELF:

WORK:

TO DO:
- [ ]
- [ ]
- [ ]
- [ ]
- [ ]
- [ ]
- [ ]
- [ ]
- [ ]
- [ ]
- [ ]
- [ ]
- [ ]
- [ ]
- [ ]
- [ ]

LAY DOWN YOUR *Sins*

LIFT UP YOUR *Wins*

Journal
RECORD NUDGES FROM DAILY DEVOTION

The Legacy Leaders like to use a popular process of P.R.A.Y. (pause, rejoice, ask, yield) after their daily Devo. As things come to you trust that it is the Holy Spirit nudging you and then do PROBLEM/WORD/GIFT/CHOICE to tap into God's help.

FREE JOURNALING OF WHATEVER IS ON YOUR MIND AS YOU THINK, LISTEN, OR WHAT WEIGHS ON YOUR MIND:

....
....
....

P (PAUSE)
....

R (REJOICE)
....

A (ASK)
....

Y (YIELD)
....
....

WAS THERE ANYTHING YOU FELT NUDGED TO WORK ON? LET'S TAP INTO THE WORD FOR HELP

PROBLEM (EXAMPLES ARE WORRY, FEAR, DOUBT, INSECURITY, IMPATIENCE)
....

WORD (GO TO THE INTERNET & LOOK UP 'MEMORY VERSES ON YOUR TOPIC & RECORD A FEW HERE)
....
....

GIFT (WRITE ABOUT WHAT LIFE WOULD LIKE BE IF YOU FOLLOW THE WORD)
....

CHOICE (YOU HAVE FREE WILL, WRITE OUT HOW YOU PLAN TO FOLLOW THROUGH)
....

MEDITATION *Verse*

(REWRITE YESTERDAY'S PROBLEM-WORD-GIFT-CHOICE MEMORY VERSE HERE)

Date: _____

| S | M | T | W | T | F | S |

MEALS:

BREAKFAST

LUNCH

DINNER

PRIORITIES:

- [ ] EXERCISED
- [ ] DEVOTIONS & JOURNAL COMPLETED

05:00
06:00
07:00
08:00
09:00
10:00
11:00
12:00
1:00
2:00
3:00
4:00
5:00
6:00
7:00
8:00
9:00

- [ ] PRAY FOR TODAY, HIS COVERING AS YOU SLEEP, AND HIS PRESENCE TOMORROW
- [ ] MOVE UNDONE TO-DO'S TO TOMORROW

WATER:
○ ○ ○
○ ○ ○

GOALS:

HOME:

SELF:

WORK:

TO DO:
- [ ]
- [ ]
- [ ]
- [ ]
- [ ]
- [ ]
- [ ]
- [ ]
- [ ]
- [ ]
- [ ]
- [ ]
- [ ]
- [ ]

LAY DOWN YOUR *Sins*

LIFT UP YOUR *Wins*

Journal
RECORD NUDGES FROM DAILY DEVOTION

The Legacy Leaders like to use a popular process of P.R.A.Y. (pause, rejoice, ask, yield) after their daily Devo. As things come to you trust that it is the Holy Spirit nudging you and then do PROBLEM/WORD/GIFT/CHOICE to tap into God's help.

FREE JOURNALING OF WHATEVER IS ON YOUR MIND AS YOU THINK, LISTEN, OR WHAT WEIGHS ON YOUR MIND:

....
....
....

P (PAUSE)
....

R (REJOICE)
....

A (ASK)
....

Y (YIELD)
....
....

WAS THERE ANYTHING YOU FELT NUDGED TO WORK ON? LET'S TAP INTO THE WORD FOR HELP

PROBLEM (EXAMPLES ARE WORRY, FEAR, DOUBT, INSECURITY, IMPATIENCE)
....

WORD (GO TO THE INTERNET & LOOK UP 'MEMORY VERSES ON YOUR TOPIC & RECORD A FEW HERE)
....
....
....

GIFT (WRITE ABOUT WHAT LIFE WOULD LIKE BE IF YOU FOLLOW THE WORD)
....

CHOICE (YOU HAVE FREE WILL, WRITE OUT HOW YOU PLAN TO FOLLOW THROUGH)
....
....

Notes

Notes

Month _____

SUN	MON	TUE	WED	THU	FRI	SAT

BIRTHDAYS/ANNIVERSARIES

_____
_____
_____

FUTURE EVENTS TO CARRY OVER

_____
_____

FULFILL YOUR LEGACY | NICCIEKLIEGL.COM | LIFE & BUSINESS COACH

FULFILL *OUR* LEGACY

Budget

MONTHLY BALANCE GOAL: _____

INCOME

DATE	SOURCE	CATEGORY	AMOUNT

BILLS & FIXED EXPENSES

DATE	SOURCE	AMOUNT

VARIABLE EXPENSES

DATE	SOURCE	AMOUNT

SUMMARY

SOURCE	AMOUNT
INCOME	
BILLS & FIXED EXPENSES	
VARIABLE EXPENSES	
BALANCE	

FULFILL YOUR LEGACY | NICCIEKLIEGL.COM | LIFE & BUSINESS COACH

FULFILL **YOUR** LEGACY

MEDITATION *Verse*

(REWRITE YESTERDAY'S PROBLEM-WORD-GIFT-CHOICE MEMORY VERSE HERE

Date: _____

| S | M | T | W | T | F | S |

MEALS:

BREAKFAST

LUNCH

DINNER

PRIORITIES:

- [ ] EXERCISED
- [ ] DEVOTIONS & JOURNAL COMPLETED

05:00
06:00
07:00
08:00
09:00
10:00
11:00
12:00
1:00
2:00
3:00
4:00
5:00
6:00
7:00
8:00
9:00

WATER:
○ ○ ○ ○
○ ○ ○ ○

GOALS:

HOME:

SELF:

WORK:

TO DO:
- [ ]
- [ ]
- [ ]
- [ ]
- [ ]
- [ ]
- [ ]
- [ ]
- [ ]
- [ ]
- [ ]
- [ ]
- [ ]
- [ ]
- [ ]

LAY DOWN YOUR *Sins*

LIFT UP YOUR *Wins*

- [ ] PRAY FOR TODAY, HIS COVERING AS YOU SLEEP, AND HIS PRESENCE TOMORROW
- [ ] MOVE UNDONE TO-DO'S TO TOMORROW

Journal
RECORD NUDGES FROM DAILY DEVOTION

The Legacy Leaders like to use a popular process of P.R.A.Y. (pause, rejoice, ask, yield) after their daily Devo. As things come to you trust that it is the Holy Spirit nudging you and then do PROBLEM/WORD/GIFT/CHOICE to tap into God's help.

FREE JOURNALING OF WHATEVER IS ON YOUR MIND AS YOU THINK, LISTEN, OR WHAT WEIGHS ON YOUR MIND:

....
....
....

P (PAUSE)
....

R (REJOICE)
....

A (ASK)
....

Y (YIELD)
....
....

WAS THERE ANYTHING YOU FELT NUDGED TO WORK ON? LET'S TAP INTO THE WORD FOR HELP

PROBLEM (EXAMPLES ARE WORRY, FEAR, DOUBT, INSECURITY, IMPATIENCE)
....

WORD (GO TO THE INTERNET & LOOK UP 'MEMORY VERSES ON YOUR TOPIC & RECORD A FEW HERE)
....
....
....

GIFT (WRITE ABOUT WHAT LIFE WOULD LIKE BE IF YOU FOLLOW THE WORD)
....

CHOICE (YOU HAVE FREE WILL, WRITE OUT HOW YOU PLAN TO FOLLOW THROUGH)
....

MEDITATION *Verse*

(REWRITE YESTERDAY'S PROBLEM-WORD-GIFT-CHOICE MEMORY VERSE HERE

Date: _____

| S | M | T | W | T | F | S |

MEALS:

BREAKFAST

LUNCH

DINNER

PRIORITIES:

- [ ] EXERCISED
- [ ] DEVOTIONS & JOURNAL COMPLETED

05:00
06:00
07:00
08:00
09:00
10:00
11:00
12:00
1:00
2:00
3:00
4:00
5:00
6:00
7:00
8:00
9:00

WATER:
○ ○ ○ ○
○ ○ ○ ○

GOALS:

HOME:

SELF:

WORK:

TO DO:
- [ ]
- [ ]
- [ ]
- [ ]
- [ ]
- [ ]
- [ ]
- [ ]
- [ ]
- [ ]
- [ ]
- [ ]
- [ ]
- [ ]

LAY DOWN YOUR *Sins*

LIFT UP YOUR *Wins*

- [ ] PRAY FOR TODAY, HIS COVERING AS YOU SLEEP, AND HIS PRESENCE TOMORROW
- [ ] MOVE UNDONE TO-DO'S TO TOMORROW

Journal
RECORD NUDGES FROM DAILY DEVOTION

The Legacy Leaders like to use a popular process of P.R.A.Y. (pause, rejoice, ask, yield) after their daily Devo. As things come to you trust that it is the Holy Spirit nudging you and then do PROBLEM/WORD/GIFT/CHOICE to tap into God's help.

FREE JOURNALING OF WHATEVER IS ON YOUR MIND AS YOU THINK, LISTEN, OR WHAT WEIGHS ON YOUR MIND:

....
....
....

P (PAUSE)
....

R (REJOICE)
....

A (ASK)
....

Y (YIELD)
....
....

WAS THERE ANYTHING YOU FELT NUDGED TO WORK ON? LET'S TAP INTO THE WORD FOR HELP

PROBLEM (EXAMPLES ARE WORRY, FEAR, DOUBT, INSECURITY, IMPATIENCE)
....

WORD (GO TO THE INTERNET & LOOK UP 'MEMORY VERSES ON YOUR TOPIC & RECORD A FEW HERE)
....
....
....

GIFT (WRITE ABOUT WHAT LIFE WOULD LIKE BE IF YOU FOLLOW THE WORD)
....

CHOICE (YOU HAVE FREE WILL, WRITE OUT HOW YOU PLAN TO FOLLOW THROUGH)
....
....

MEDITATION *Verse*

(REWRITE YESTERDAY'S PROBLEM-WORD-GIFT-CHOICE MEMORY VERSE HERE)

Date: _____

| S | M | T | W | T | F | S |

MEALS:

BREAKFAST

LUNCH

DINNER

PRIORITIES:

☐ EXERCISED
☐ DEVOTIONS & JOURNAL COMPLETED

- 05:00
- 06:00
- 07:00
- 08:00
- 09:00
- 10:00
- 11:00
- 12:00
- 1:00
- 2:00
- 3:00
- 4:00
- 5:00
- 6:00
- 7:00
- 8:00
- 9:00

WATER:
○ ○ ○
○ ○ ○

GOALS:

HOME:

SELF:

WORK:

TO DO:
☐
☐
☐
☐
☐
☐
☐
☐
☐
☐
☐
☐
☐
☐
☐
☐
☐

LAY DOWN YOUR *Sins*

LIFT UP YOUR *Wins*

☐ PRAY FOR TODAY, HIS COVERING AS YOU SLEEP, AND HIS PRESENCE TOMORROW
☐ MOVE UNDONE TO-DO'S TO TOMORROW

Journal
RECORD NUDGES FROM DAILY DEVOTION

The Legacy Leaders like to use a popular process of P.R.A.Y. (pause, rejoice, ask, yield) after their daily Devo. As things come to you trust that it is the Holy Spirit nudging you and then do PROBLEM/WORD/GIFT/CHOICE to tap into God's help.

<u>FREE JOURNALING OF WHATEVER IS ON YOUR MIND AS YOU THINK, LISTEN, OR WHAT WEIGHS ON YOUR MIND:</u>

....
....
....

P (PAUSE)
....

R (REJOICE)
....

A (ASK)
....

Y (YIELD)
....
....

<u>WAS THERE ANYTHING YOU FELT NUDGED TO WORK ON? LET'S TAP INTO THE WORD FOR HELP</u>

PROBLEM (EXAMPLES ARE WORRY, FEAR, DOUBT, INSECURITY, IMPATIENCE)
....

WORD (GO TO THE INTERNET & LOOK UP 'MEMORY VERSES ON YOUR TOPIC & RECORD A FEW HERE)
....
....

GIFT (WRITE ABOUT WHAT LIFE WOULD LIKE BE IF YOU FOLLOW THE WORD)
....

CHOICE (YOU HAVE FREE WILL, WRITE OUT HOW YOU PLAN TO FOLLOW THROUGH)
....

MEDITATION *Verse*

(REWRITE YESTERDAY'S PROBLEM-WORD-GIFT-CHOICE MEMORY VERSE HERE)

Date: _____

| S | M | T | W | T | F | S |

MEALS:

BREAKFAST

LUNCH

DINNER

PRIORITIES:

- [ ] EXERCISED
- [ ] DEVOTIONS & JOURNAL COMPLETED

05:00
06:00
07:00
08:00
09:00
10:00
11:00
12:00
1:00
2:00
3:00
4:00
5:00
6:00
7:00
8:00
9:00

WATER:
○ ○ ○ ○
○ ○ ○ ○

GOALS:

HOME:

SELF:

WORK:

TO DO:
- [ ]
- [ ]
- [ ]
- [ ]
- [ ]
- [ ]
- [ ]
- [ ]
- [ ]
- [ ]
- [ ]
- [ ]
- [ ]
- [ ]
- [ ]

LAY DOWN YOUR *Sins*

LIFT UP YOUR *Wins*

- [ ] PRAY FOR TODAY, HIS COVERING AS YOU SLEEP, AND HIS PRESENCE TOMORROW
- [ ] MOVE UNDONE TO-DO'S TO TOMORROW

Journal
RECORD NUDGES FROM DAILY DEVOTION

The Legacy Leaders like to use a popular process of P.R.A.Y. (pause, rejoice, ask, yield) after their daily Devo. As things come to you trust that it is the Holy Spirit nudging you and then do PROBLEM/WORD/GIFT/CHOICE to tap into God's help.

FREE JOURNALING OF WHATEVER IS ON YOUR MIND AS YOU THINK, LISTEN, OR WHAT WEIGHS ON YOUR MIND:

P (PAUSE)

R (REJOICE)

A (ASK)

Y (YIELD)

WAS THERE ANYTHING YOU FELT NUDGED TO WORK ON? LET'S TAP INTO THE WORD FOR HELP

PROBLEM (EXAMPLES ARE WORRY, FEAR, DOUBT, INSECURITY, IMPATIENCE)

WORD (GO TO THE INTERNET & LOOK UP 'MEMORY VERSES ON YOUR TOPIC & RECORD A FEW HERE)

GIFT (WRITE ABOUT WHAT LIFE WOULD LIKE BE IF YOU FOLLOW THE WORD)

CHOICE (YOU HAVE FREE WILL, WRITE OUT HOW YOU PLAN TO FOLLOW THROUGH)

MEDITATION *Verse*

(REWRITE YESTERDAY'S PROBLEM-WORD-GIFT-CHOICE MEMORY VERSE HERE

Date: _____

| S | M | T | W | T | F | S |

MEALS:

BREAKFAST

LUNCH

DINNER

PRIORITIES:

- [ ] EXERCISED
- [ ] DEVOTIONS & JOURNAL COMPLETED

05:00
06:00
07:00
08:00
09:00
10:00
11:00
12:00
1:00
2:00
3:00
4:00
5:00
6:00
7:00
8:00
9:00

WATER:
○ ○ ○ ○
○ ○ ○ ○

GOALS:

HOME:

SELF:

WORK:

TO DO:
- [ ]
- [ ]
- [ ]
- [ ]
- [ ]
- [ ]
- [ ]
- [ ]
- [ ]
- [ ]
- [ ]
- [ ]
- [ ]
- [ ]
- [ ]

LAY DOWN YOUR *Sins*

LIFT UP YOUR *Wins*

- [ ] PRAY FOR TODAY, HIS COVERING AS YOU SLEEP, AND HIS PRESENCE TOMORROW
- [ ] MOVE UNDONE TO-DO'S TO TOMORROW

Journal
RECORD NUDGES FROM DAILY DEVOTION

The Legacy Leaders like to use a popular process of P.R.A.Y. (pause, rejoice, ask, yield) after their daily Devo. As things come to you trust that it is the Holy Spirit nudging you and then do PROBLEM/WORD/GIFT/CHOICE to tap into God's help.

FREE JOURNALING OF WHATEVER IS ON YOUR MIND AS YOU THINK, LISTEN, OR WHAT WEIGHS ON YOUR MIND:

....
....
....

P (PAUSE)
....

R (REJOICE)
....

A (ASK)
....

Y (YIELD)
....
....

WAS THERE ANYTHING YOU FELT NUDGED TO WORK ON? LET'S TAP INTO THE WORD FOR HELP

PROBLEM (EXAMPLES ARE WORRY, FEAR, DOUBT, INSECURITY, IMPATIENCE)
....

WORD (GO TO THE INTERNET & LOOK UP 'MEMORY VERSES ON YOUR TOPIC & RECORD A FEW HERE)
....
....
....

GIFT (WRITE ABOUT WHAT LIFE WOULD LIKE BE IF YOU FOLLOW THE WORD)
....

CHOICE (YOU HAVE FREE WILL, WRITE OUT HOW YOU PLAN TO FOLLOW THROUGH)
....
....

MEDITATION *Verse*

[REWRITE YESTERDAY'S PROBLEM-WORD-GIFT-CHOICE MEMORY VERSE HERE

Date: _____

| S | M | T | W | T | F | S |

MEALS:

BREAKFAST

LUNCH

DINNER

PRIORITIES:
- [ ] EXERCISED
- [ ] DEVOTIONS & JOURNAL COMPLETED

05:00
06:00
07:00
08:00
09:00
10:00
11:00
12:00
1:00
2:00
3:00
4:00
5:00
6:00
7:00
8:00
9:00

WATER:
○ ○ ○
○ ○ ○

GOALS:

HOME:

SELF:

WORK:

TO DO:
- [ ]
- [ ]
- [ ]
- [ ]
- [ ]
- [ ]
- [ ]
- [ ]
- [ ]
- [ ]
- [ ]
- [ ]
- [ ]
- [ ]
- [ ]
- [ ]

LAY DOWN YOUR *Sins*

LIFT UP YOUR *Wins*

- [ ] PRAY FOR TODAY, HIS COVERING AS YOU SLEEP, AND HIS PRESENCE TOMORROW
- [ ] MOVE UNDONE TO-DO'S TO TOMORROW

Journal
RECORD NUDGES FROM DAILY DEVOTION

The Legacy Leaders like to use a popular process of P.R.A.Y. (pause, rejoice, ask, yield) after their daily Devo. As things come to you trust that it is the Holy Spirit nudging you and then do PROBLEM/WORD/GIFT/CHOICE to tap into God's help.

FREE JOURNALING OF WHATEVER IS ON YOUR MIND AS YOU THINK, LISTEN, OR WHAT WEIGHS ON YOUR MIND:

....
....
....

P (PAUSE)
....

R (REJOICE)
....

A (ASK)
....

Y (YIELD)
....
....

WAS THERE ANYTHING YOU FELT NUDGED TO WORK ON? LET'S TAP INTO THE WORD FOR HELP

PROBLEM (EXAMPLES ARE WORRY, FEAR, DOUBT, INSECURITY, IMPATIENCE)
....

WORD (GO TO THE INTERNET & LOOK UP 'MEMORY VERSES ON YOUR TOPIC & RECORD A FEW HERE)
....
....

GIFT (WRITE ABOUT WHAT LIFE WOULD LIKE BE IF YOU FOLLOW THE WORD)
....

CHOICE (YOU HAVE FREE WILL, WRITE OUT HOW YOU PLAN TO FOLLOW THROUGH)
....
....

MEDITATION *Verse*

(REWRITE YESTERDAY'S PROBLEM-WORD-GIFT-CHOICE MEMORY VERSE HERE)

Date: _____

| S | M | T | W | T | F | S |

MEALS:

BREAKFAST

LUNCH

DINNER

PRIORITIES:

☐ EXERCISED
☐ DEVOTIONS & JOURNAL COMPLETED

05:00
06:00
07:00
08:00
09:00
10:00
11:00
12:00
1:00
2:00
3:00
4:00
5:00
6:00
7:00
8:00
9:00

☐ PRAY FOR TODAY, HIS COVERING AS YOU SLEEP, AND HIS PRESENCE TOMORROW
☐ MOVE UNDONE TO-DO'S TO TOMORROW

WATER:
○ ○ ○ ○
○ ○ ○ ○

GOALS:

HOME:

SELF:

WORK:

TO DO:
☐
☐
☐
☐
☐
☐
☐
☐
☐
☐
☐
☐
☐
☐
☐

LAY DOWN YOUR *Sins*

LIFT UP YOUR *Wins*

Journal
RECORD NUDGES FROM DAILY DEVOTION

The Legacy Leaders like to use a popular process of P.R.A.Y. (pause, rejoice, ask, yield) after their daily Devo. As things come to you trust that it is the Holy Spirit nudging you and then do PROBLEM/WORD/GIFT/CHOICE to tap into God's help.

FREE JOURNALING OF WHATEVER IS ON YOUR MIND AS YOU THINK, LISTEN, OR WHAT WEIGHS ON YOUR MIND:

P (PAUSE)

R (REJOICE)

A (ASK)

Y (YIELD)

WAS THERE ANYTHING YOU FELT NUDGED TO WORK ON? LET'S TAP INTO THE WORD FOR HELP

PROBLEM (EXAMPLES ARE WORRY, FEAR, DOUBT, INSECURITY, IMPATIENCE)

WORD (GO TO THE INTERNET & LOOK UP 'MEMORY VERSES ON YOUR TOPIC & RECORD A FEW HERE)

GIFT (WRITE ABOUT WHAT LIFE WOULD LIKE BE IF YOU FOLLOW THE WORD)

CHOICE (YOU HAVE FREE WILL, WRITE OUT HOW YOU PLAN TO FOLLOW THROUGH)

MEDITATION *Verse*

(REWRITE YESTERDAY'S PROBLEM-WORD-GIFT-CHOICE MEMORY VERSE HERE

Date: _____

| S | M | T | W | T | F | S |

MEALS:

BREAKFAST

LUNCH

DINNER

PRIORITIES:

- [ ] EXERCISED
- [ ] DEVOTIONS & JOURNAL COMPLETED

05:00
06:00
07:00
08:00
09:00
10:00
11:00
12:00
1:00
2:00
3:00
4:00
5:00
6:00
7:00
8:00
9:00

- [ ] PRAY FOR TODAY, HIS COVERING AS YOU SLEEP, AND HIS PRESENCE TOMORROW
- [ ] MOVE UNDONE TO-DO'S TO TOMORROW

WATER:
○ ○ ○ ○
○ ○ ○ ○

GOALS:

HOME:

SELF:

WORK:

TO DO:
- [ ]
- [ ]
- [ ]
- [ ]
- [ ]
- [ ]
- [ ]
- [ ]
- [ ]
- [ ]
- [ ]
- [ ]
- [ ]
- [ ]

LAY DOWN YOUR *Sins*

LIFT UP YOUR *Wins*

Journal
RECORD NUDGES FROM DAILY DEVOTION

The Legacy Leaders like to use a popular process of P.R.A.Y. (pause, rejoice, ask, yield) after their daily Devo. As things come to you trust that it is the Holy Spirit nudging you and then do PROBLEM/WORD/GIFT/CHOICE to tap into God's help.

FREE JOURNALING OF WHATEVER IS ON YOUR MIND AS YOU THINK, LISTEN, OR WHAT WEIGHS ON YOUR MIND:

....
....
....

P (PAUSE)
....

R (REJOICE)
....

A (ASK)
....

Y (YIELD)
....
....

WAS THERE ANYTHING YOU FELT NUDGED TO WORK ON? LET'S TAP INTO THE WORD FOR HELP

PROBLEM (EXAMPLES ARE WORRY, FEAR, DOUBT, INSECURITY, IMPATIENCE)
....

WORD (GO TO THE INTERNET & LOOK UP 'MEMORY VERSES ON YOUR TOPIC & RECORD A FEW HERE)
....
....
....

GIFT (WRITE ABOUT WHAT LIFE WOULD LIKE BE IF YOU FOLLOW THE WORD)
....

CHOICE (YOU HAVE FREE WILL, WRITE OUT HOW YOU PLAN TO FOLLOW THROUGH)
....

MEDITATION *Verse*

(REWRITE YESTERDAY'S PROBLEM-WORD-GIFT-CHOICE MEMORY VERSE HERE)

Date: _____

| S | M | T | W | T | F | S |

MEALS:

BREAKFAST

LUNCH

DINNER

PRIORITIES:

☐ EXERCISED
☐ DEVOTIONS & JOURNAL COMPLETED

05:00
06:00
07:00
08:00
09:00
10:00
11:00
12:00
1:00
2:00
3:00
4:00
5:00
6:00
7:00
8:00
9:00

WATER:
○ ○ ○ ○
○ ○ ○ ○

GOALS:

HOME:

SELF:

WORK:

TO DO:
☐
☐
☐
☐
☐
☐
☐
☐
☐
☐
☐
☐
☐
☐
☐

LAY DOWN YOUR *Sins*

LIFT UP YOUR *Wins*

☐ PRAY FOR TODAY, HIS COVERING AS YOU SLEEP, AND HIS PRESENCE TOMORROW
☐ MOVE UNDONE TO-DO'S TO TOMORROW

Journal
RECORD NUDGES FROM DAILY DEVOTION

The Legacy Leaders like to use a popular process of P.R.A.Y. (pause, rejoice, ask, yield) after their daily Devo. As things come to you trust that it is the Holy Spirit nudging you and then do PROBLEM/WORD/GIFT/CHOICE to tap into God's help.

FREE JOURNALING OF WHATEVER IS ON YOUR MIND AS YOU THINK, LISTEN, OR WHAT WEIGHS ON YOUR MIND:

....

....

....

P (PAUSE)
....

R (REJOICE)
....

A (ASK)
....

Y (YIELD)
....

WAS THERE ANYTHING YOU FELT NUDGED TO WORK ON? LET'S TAP INTO THE WORD FOR HELP

PROBLEM (EXAMPLES ARE WORRY, FEAR, DOUBT, INSECURITY, IMPATIENCE)
....

WORD (GO TO THE INTERNET & LOOK UP 'MEMORY VERSES ON YOUR TOPIC & RECORD A FEW HERE)
....
....
....

GIFT (WRITE ABOUT WHAT LIFE WOULD LIKE BE IF YOU FOLLOW THE WORD)
....

CHOICE (YOU HAVE FREE WILL, WRITE OUT HOW YOU PLAN TO FOLLOW THROUGH)
....

MEDITATION *Verse*

(REWRITE YESTERDAY'S PROBLEM-WORD-GIFT-CHOICE MEMORY VERSE HERE)

Date: _____

S	M	T	W	T	F	S

MEALS:

BREAKFAST

LUNCH

DINNER

PRIORITIES:

- [ ] EXERCISED
- [ ] DEVOTIONS & JOURNAL COMPLETED

- 05:00
- 06:00
- 07:00
- 08:00
- 09:00
- 10:00
- 11:00
- 12:00
- 1:00
- 2:00
- 3:00
- 4:00
- 5:00
- 6:00
- 7:00
- 8:00
- 9:00

WATER:
○ ○ ○ ○
○ ○ ○ ○

GOALS:

HOME:

SELF:

WORK:

TO DO:
- [ ]
- [ ]
- [ ]
- [ ]
- [ ]
- [ ]
- [ ]
- [ ]
- [ ]
- [ ]
- [ ]
- [ ]
- [ ]
- [ ]

LAY DOWN YOUR *Sins*

LIFT UP YOUR *Wins*

- [ ] PRAY FOR TODAY, HIS COVERING AS YOU SLEEP, AND HIS PRESENCE TOMORROW
- [ ] MOVE UNDONE TO-DO'S TO TOMORROW

Journal
RECORD NUDGES FROM DAILY DEVOTION

The Legacy Leaders like to use a popular process of P.R.A.Y. (pause, rejoice, ask, yield) after their daily Devo. As things come to you trust that it is the Holy Spirit nudging you and then do PROBLEM/WORD/GIFT/CHOICE to tap into God's help.

FREE JOURNALING OF WHATEVER IS ON YOUR MIND AS YOU THINK, LISTEN, OR WHAT WEIGHS ON YOUR MIND:

....
....
....

P (PAUSE)
....

R (REJOICE)
....

A (ASK)
....

Y (YIELD)
....
....

WAS THERE ANYTHING YOU FELT NUDGED TO WORK ON? LET'S TAP INTO THE WORD FOR HELP

PROBLEM (EXAMPLES ARE WORRY, FEAR, DOUBT, INSECURITY, IMPATIENCE)
....

WORD (GO TO THE INTERNET & LOOK UP 'MEMORY VERSES ON YOUR TOPIC & RECORD A FEW HERE)
....
....
....

GIFT (WRITE ABOUT WHAT LIFE WOULD LIKE BE IF YOU FOLLOW THE WORD)
....

CHOICE (YOU HAVE FREE WILL, WRITE OUT HOW YOU PLAN TO FOLLOW THROUGH)
....
....

MEDITATION *Verse*

(REWRITE YESTERDAY'S PROBLEM-WORD-GIFT-CHOICE MEMORY VERSE HERE

Date: _____

| S | M | T | W | T | F | S |

MEALS:

BREAKFAST

LUNCH

DINNER

PRIORITIES:

- [ ] EXERCISED
- [ ] DEVOTIONS & JOURNAL COMPLETED

05:00
06:00
07:00
08:00
09:00
10:00
11:00
12:00
1:00
2:00
3:00
4:00
5:00
6:00
7:00
8:00
9:00

WATER:
○ ○ ○ ○
○ ○ ○ ○

GOALS:

HOME:

SELF:

WORK:

TO DO:
- [ ]
- [ ]
- [ ]
- [ ]
- [ ]
- [ ]
- [ ]
- [ ]
- [ ]
- [ ]
- [ ]
- [ ]
- [ ]
- [ ]
- [ ]
- [ ]
- [ ]

LAY DOWN YOUR *Sins*

LIFT UP YOUR *Wins*

- [ ] PRAY FOR TODAY, HIS COVERING AS YOU SLEEP, AND HIS PRESENCE TOMORROW
- [ ] MOVE UNDONE TO-DO'S TO TOMORROW

Journal
RECORD NUDGES FROM DAILY DEVOTION

The Legacy Leaders like to use a popular process of P.R.A.Y. (pause, rejoice, ask, yield) after their daily Devo. As things come to you trust that it is the Holy Spirit nudging you and then do PROBLEM/WORD/GIFT/CHOICE to tap into God's help.

FREE JOURNALING OF WHATEVER IS ON YOUR MIND AS YOU THINK, LISTEN, OR WHAT WEIGHS ON YOUR MIND:

....
....
....

P (PAUSE)
....

R (REJOICE)
....

A (ASK)
....

Y (YIELD)
....
....

WAS THERE ANYTHING YOU FELT NUDGED TO WORK ON? LET'S TAP INTO THE WORD FOR HELP

PROBLEM (EXAMPLES ARE WORRY, FEAR, DOUBT, INSECURITY, IMPATIENCE)
....

WORD (GO TO THE INTERNET & LOOK UP 'MEMORY VERSES ON YOUR TOPIC & RECORD A FEW HERE)
....
....
....

GIFT (WRITE ABOUT WHAT LIFE WOULD LIKE BE IF YOU FOLLOW THE WORD)
....

CHOICE (YOU HAVE FREE WILL, WRITE OUT HOW YOU PLAN TO FOLLOW THROUGH)
....
....

MEDITATION *Verse*

(REWRITE YESTERDAY'S PROBLEM-WORD-GIFT-CHOICE MEMORY VERSE HERE)

Date:_____

| S | M | T | W | T | F | S |

MEALS:

BREAKFAST

LUNCH

DINNER

PRIORITIES:

☐ EXERCISED
☐ DEVOTIONS & JOURNAL COMPLETED

05:00
06:00
07:00
08:00
09:00
10:00
11:00
12:00
1:00
2:00
3:00
4:00
5:00
6:00
7:00
8:00
9:00

☐ PRAY FOR TODAY, HIS COVERING AS YOU SLEEP, AND HIS PRESENCE TOMORROW
☐ MOVE UNDONE TO-DO'S TO TOMORROW

WATER:
○ ○ ○ ○
○ ○ ○ ○

GOALS:

HOME:

SELF:

WORK:

TO DO:
☐
☐
☐
☐
☐
☐
☐
☐
☐
☐
☐
☐
☐
☐
☐
☐

LAY DOWN YOUR *Sins*

LIFT UP YOUR *Wins*

Journal
RECORD NUDGES FROM DAILY DEVOTION

The Legacy Leaders like to use a popular process of P.R.A.Y. (pause, rejoice, ask, yield) after their daily Devo. As things come to you trust that it is the Holy Spirit nudging you and then do PROBLEM/WORD/GIFT/CHOICE to tap into God's help.

FREE JOURNALING OF WHATEVER IS ON YOUR MIND AS YOU THINK, LISTEN, OR WHAT WEIGHS ON YOUR MIND:

....
....
....

P (PAUSE)
....

R (REJOICE)
....

A (ASK)
....

Y (YIELD)
....
....

WAS THERE ANYTHING YOU FELT NUDGED TO WORK ON? LET'S TAP INTO THE WORD FOR HELP

PROBLEM (EXAMPLES ARE WORRY, FEAR, DOUBT, INSECURITY, IMPATIENCE)
....

WORD (GO TO THE INTERNET & LOOK UP 'MEMORY VERSES ON YOUR TOPIC & RECORD A FEW HERE)
....
....
....

GIFT (WRITE ABOUT WHAT LIFE WOULD LIKE BE IF YOU FOLLOW THE WORD)
....

CHOICE (YOU HAVE FREE WILL, WRITE OUT HOW YOU PLAN TO FOLLOW THROUGH)
....
....

MEDITATION *Verse*

(REWRITE YESTERDAY'S PROBLEM-WORD-GIFT-CHOICE MEMORY VERSE HERE

Date: _____
| S | M | T | W | T | F | S |

MEALS:

BREAKFAST

LUNCH

DINNER

PRIORITIES:
- [ ] EXERCISED
- [ ] DEVOTIONS & JOURNAL COMPLETED

05:00
06:00
07:00
08:00
09:00
10:00
11:00
12:00
1:00
2:00
3:00
4:00
5:00
6:00
7:00
8:00
9:00

- [ ] PRAY FOR TODAY, HIS COVERING AS YOU SLEEP, AND HIS PRESENCE TOMORROW
- [ ] MOVE UNDONE TO-DO'S TO TOMORROW

WATER:
○ ○ ○ ○
○ ○ ○ ○

GOALS:

HOME:

SELF:

WORK:

TO DO:
- [ ]
- [ ]
- [ ]
- [ ]
- [ ]
- [ ]
- [ ]
- [ ]
- [ ]
- [ ]
- [ ]
- [ ]
- [ ]
- [ ]

LAY DOWN YOUR *Sins*

LIFT UP YOUR *Wins*

Journal
RECORD NUDGES FROM DAILY DEVOTION

The Legacy Leaders like to use a popular process of P.R.A.Y. (pause, rejoice, ask, yield) after their daily Devo. As things come to you trust that it is the Holy Spirit nudging you and then do PROBLEM/WORD/GIFT/CHOICE to tap into God's help.

FREE JOURNALING OF WHATEVER IS ON YOUR MIND AS YOU THINK, LISTEN, OR WHAT WEIGHS ON YOUR MIND:

....
....
....

P (PAUSE)
....

R (REJOICE)
....

A (ASK)
....

Y (YIELD)
....
....

WAS THERE ANYTHING YOU FELT NUDGED TO WORK ON? LET'S TAP INTO THE WORD FOR HELP

PROBLEM (EXAMPLES ARE WORRY, FEAR, DOUBT, INSECURITY, IMPATIENCE)
....

WORD (GO TO THE INTERNET & LOOK UP 'MEMORY VERSES ON YOUR TOPIC & RECORD A FEW HERE)
....
....
....

GIFT (WRITE ABOUT WHAT LIFE WOULD LIKE BE IF YOU FOLLOW THE WORD)
....

CHOICE (YOU HAVE FREE WILL, WRITE OUT HOW YOU PLAN TO FOLLOW THROUGH)
....
....

MEDITATION *Verse*

(REWRITE YESTERDAY'S PROBLEM-WORD-GIFT-CHOICE MEMORY VERSE HERE

Date: _____

| S | M | T | W | T | F | S |

MEALS:

BREAKFAST

LUNCH

DINNER

PRIORITIES:

☐ EXERCISED
☐ DEVOTIONS & JOURNAL COMPLETED

05:00
06:00
07:00
08:00
09:00
10:00
11:00
12:00
1:00
2:00
3:00
4:00
5:00
6:00
7:00
8:00
9:00

☐ PRAY FOR TODAY, HIS COVERING AS YOU SLEEP, AND HIS PRESENCE TOMORROW
☐ MOVE UNDONE TO-DO'S TO TOMORROW

WATER:
○ ○ ○ ○
○ ○ ○ ○

GOALS:

HOME:

SELF:

WORK:

TO DO:
☐
☐
☐
☐
☐
☐
☐
☐
☐
☐
☐
☐
☐
☐

LAY DOWN YOUR *Sins*

LIFT UP YOUR *Wins*

Journal
RECORD NUDGES FROM DAILY DEVOTION

The Legacy Leaders like to use a popular process of P.R.A.Y. (pause, rejoice, ask, yield) after their daily Devo. As things come to you trust that it is the Holy Spirit nudging you and then do PROBLEM/WORD/GIFT/CHOICE to tap into God's help.

FREE JOURNALING OF WHATEVER IS ON YOUR MIND AS YOU THINK, LISTEN, OR WHAT WEIGHS ON YOUR MIND:

....
....
....

P (PAUSE)
....

R (REJOICE)
....

A (ASK)
....

Y (YIELD)
....
....

WAS THERE ANYTHING YOU FELT NUDGED TO WORK ON? LET'S TAP INTO THE WORD FOR HELP

PROBLEM (EXAMPLES ARE WORRY, FEAR, DOUBT, INSECURITY, IMPATIENCE)
....

WORD (GO TO THE INTERNET & LOOK UP 'MEMORY VERSES ON YOUR TOPIC & RECORD A FEW HERE)
....
....
....

GIFT (WRITE ABOUT WHAT LIFE WOULD LIKE BE IF YOU FOLLOW THE WORD)
....

CHOICE (YOU HAVE FREE WILL, WRITE OUT HOW YOU PLAN TO FOLLOW THROUGH)
....

MEDITATION *Verse*

(REWRITE YESTERDAY'S PROBLEM-WORD-GIFT-CHOICE MEMORY VERSE HERE)

Date: _____

| S | M | T | W | T | F | S |

MEALS:

BREAKFAST

LUNCH

DINNER

PRIORITIES:

- [ ] EXERCISED
- [ ] DEVOTIONS & JOURNAL COMPLETED

05:00
06:00
07:00
08:00
09:00
10:00
11:00
12:00
1:00
2:00
3:00
4:00
5:00
6:00
7:00
8:00
9:00

- [ ] PRAY FOR TODAY, HIS COVERING AS YOU SLEEP, AND HIS PRESENCE TOMORROW
- [ ] MOVE UNDONE TO-DO'S TO TOMORROW

WATER:
○ ○ ○
○ ○ ○

GOALS:

HOME:

SELF:

WORK:

TO DO:
- [ ]
- [ ]
- [ ]
- [ ]
- [ ]
- [ ]
- [ ]
- [ ]
- [ ]
- [ ]
- [ ]
- [ ]
- [ ]
- [ ]

LAY DOWN YOUR *Sins*

LIFT UP YOUR *Wins*

Journal
RECORD NUDGES FROM DAILY DEVOTION

The Legacy Leaders like to use a popular process of P.R.A.Y. (pause, rejoice, ask, yield) after their daily Devo. As things come to you trust that it is the Holy Spirit nudging you and then do PROBLEM/WORD/GIFT/CHOICE to tap into God's help.

FREE JOURNALING OF WHATEVER IS ON YOUR MIND AS YOU THINK, LISTEN, OR WHAT WEIGHS ON YOUR MIND:

....
....
....

P (PAUSE)
....

R (REJOICE)
....

A (ASK)
....

Y (YIELD)
....
....

WAS THERE ANYTHING YOU FELT NUDGED TO WORK ON? LET'S TAP INTO THE WORD FOR HELP

PROBLEM (EXAMPLES ARE WORRY, FEAR, DOUBT, INSECURITY, IMPATIENCE)
....

WORD (GO TO THE INTERNET & LOOK UP 'MEMORY VERSES ON YOUR TOPIC & RECORD A FEW HERE)
....
....

GIFT (WRITE ABOUT WHAT LIFE WOULD LIKE BE IF YOU FOLLOW THE WORD)
....

CHOICE (YOU HAVE FREE WILL, WRITE OUT HOW YOU PLAN TO FOLLOW THROUGH)
....

MEDITATION *Verse*

(REWRITE YESTERDAY'S PROBLEM-WORD-GIFT-CHOICE MEMORY VERSE HERE

Date: _____

| S | M | T | W | T | F | S |

MEALS:

BREAKFAST

LUNCH

DINNER

PRIORITIES:

- [ ] EXERCISED
- [ ] DEVOTIONS & JOURNAL COMPLETED

05:00
06:00
07:00
08:00
09:00
10:00
11:00
12:00
1:00
2:00
3:00
4:00
5:00
6:00
7:00
8:00
9:00

WATER:
○ ○ ○ ○
○ ○ ○ ○

GOALS:

HOME:

SELF:

WORK:

TO DO:

LAY DOWN YOUR *Sins*

LIFT UP YOUR *Wins*

- [ ] PRAY FOR TODAY, HIS COVERING AS YOU SLEEP, AND HIS PRESENCE TOMORROW
- [ ] MOVE UNDONE TO-DO'S TO TOMORROW

Journal
RECORD NUDGES FROM DAILY DEVOTION

The Legacy Leaders like to use a popular process of P.R.A.Y. (pause, rejoice, ask, yield) after their daily Devo. As things come to you trust that it is the Holy Spirit nudging you and then do PROBLEM/WORD/GIFT/CHOICE to tap into God's help.

FREE JOURNALING OF WHATEVER IS ON YOUR MIND AS YOU THINK, LISTEN, OR WHAT WEIGHS ON YOUR MIND:

....
....
....
....

P (PAUSE)
....

R (REJOICE)
....

A (ASK)
....

Y (YIELD)
....
....

WAS THERE ANYTHING YOU FELT NUDGED TO WORK ON? LET'S TAP INTO THE WORD FOR HELP

PROBLEM (EXAMPLES ARE WORRY, FEAR, DOUBT, INSECURITY, IMPATIENCE)
....

WORD (GO TO THE INTERNET & LOOK UP 'MEMORY VERSES ON YOUR TOPIC & RECORD A FEW HERE)
....
....
....

GIFT (WRITE ABOUT WHAT LIFE WOULD LIKE BE IF YOU FOLLOW THE WORD)
....
....

CHOICE (YOU HAVE FREE WILL, WRITE OUT HOW YOU PLAN TO FOLLOW THROUGH)
....
....

MEDITATION *Verse*

(REWRITE YESTERDAY'S PROBLEM-WORD-GIFT-CHOICE MEMORY VERSE HERE

Date: _____

| S | M | T | W | T | F | S |

MEALS:

BREAKFAST

LUNCH

DINNER

PRIORITIES:

- [ ] EXERCISED
- [ ] DEVOTIONS & JOURNAL COMPLETED

05:00
06:00
07:00
08:00
09:00
10:00
11:00
12:00
1:00
2:00
3:00
4:00
5:00
6:00
7:00
8:00
9:00

- [ ] PRAY FOR TODAY, HIS COVERING AS YOU SLEEP, AND HIS PRESENCE TOMORROW
- [ ] MOVE UNDONE TO-DO'S TO TOMORROW

WATER:
○ ○ ○ ○
○ ○ ○ ○

GOALS:

HOME:

SELF:

WORK:

TO DO:
- [ ]
- [ ]
- [ ]
- [ ]
- [ ]
- [ ]
- [ ]
- [ ]
- [ ]
- [ ]
- [ ]
- [ ]
- [ ]
- [ ]
- [ ]
- [ ]
- [ ]

LAY DOWN YOUR *Sins*

LIFT UP YOUR *Wins*

Journal
RECORD NUDGES FROM DAILY DEVOTION

The Legacy Leaders like to use a popular process of P.R.A.Y. (pause, rejoice, ask, yield) after their daily Devo. As things come to you trust that it is the Holy Spirit nudging you and then do PROBLEM/WORD/GIFT/CHOICE to tap into God's help.

FREE JOURNALING OF WHATEVER IS ON YOUR MIND AS YOU THINK, LISTEN, OR WHAT WEIGHS ON YOUR MIND:

....

....

....

P (PAUSE)
....

R (REJOICE)
....

A (ASK)
....

Y (YIELD)
....

....

WAS THERE ANYTHING YOU FELT NUDGED TO WORK ON? LET'S TAP INTO THE WORD FOR HELP

PROBLEM (EXAMPLES ARE WORRY, FEAR, DOUBT, INSECURITY, IMPATIENCE)
....

WORD (GO TO THE INTERNET & LOOK UP 'MEMORY VERSES ON YOUR TOPIC & RECORD A FEW HERE)
....

....

....

GIFT (WRITE ABOUT WHAT LIFE WOULD LIKE BE IF YOU FOLLOW THE WORD)
....

CHOICE (YOU HAVE FREE WILL, WRITE OUT HOW YOU PLAN TO FOLLOW THROUGH)
....

....

MEDITATION *Verse*

(REWRITE YESTERDAY'S PROBLEM-WORD-GIFT-CHOICE MEMORY VERSE HERE)

Date: _____

| S | M | T | W | T | F | S |

MEALS:

BREAKFAST

LUNCH

DINNER

PRIORITIES:

☐ EXERCISED
☐ DEVOTIONS & JOURNAL COMPLETED

05:00
06:00
07:00
08:00
09:00
10:00
11:00
12:00
1:00
2:00
3:00
4:00
5:00
6:00
7:00
8:00
9:00

☐ PRAY FOR TODAY, HIS COVERING AS YOU SLEEP, AND HIS PRESENCE TOMORROW
☐ MOVE UNDONE TO-DO'S TO TOMORROW

WATER:
○ ○ ○
○ ○ ○

GOALS:

HOME:

SELF:

WORK:

TO DO:
☐
☐
☐
☐
☐
☐
☐
☐
☐
☐
☐
☐
☐
☐
☐
☐

LAY DOWN YOUR *Sins*

LIFT UP YOUR *Wins*

Journal
RECORD NUDGES FROM DAILY DEVOTION

The Legacy Leaders like to use a popular process of P.R.A.Y. (pause, rejoice, ask, yield) after their daily Devo. As things come to you trust that it is the Holy Spirit nudging you and then do PROBLEM/WORD/GIFT/CHOICE to tap into God's help.

FREE JOURNALING OF WHATEVER IS ON YOUR MIND AS YOU THINK, LISTEN, OR WHAT WEIGHS ON YOUR MIND:

....
....
....

P (PAUSE)
....

R (REJOICE)
....

A (ASK)
....

Y (YIELD)
....
....

WAS THERE ANYTHING YOU FELT NUDGED TO WORK ON? LET'S TAP INTO THE WORD FOR HELP

PROBLEM (EXAMPLES ARE WORRY, FEAR, DOUBT, INSECURITY, IMPATIENCE)
....

WORD (GO TO THE INTERNET & LOOK UP 'MEMORY VERSES ON YOUR TOPIC & RECORD A FEW HERE)
....
....
....

GIFT (WRITE ABOUT WHAT LIFE WOULD LIKE BE IF YOU FOLLOW THE WORD)
....
....

CHOICE (YOU HAVE FREE WILL. WRITE OUT HOW YOU PLAN TO FOLLOW THROUGH)
....
....

MEDITATION *Verse*

(REWRITE YESTERDAY'S PROBLEM-WORD-GIFT-CHOICE MEMORY VERSE HERE)

Date: _____

| S | M | T | W | T | F | S |

MEALS:

BREAKFAST

LUNCH

DINNER

PRIORITIES:

- [ ] EXERCISED
- [ ] DEVOTIONS & JOURNAL COMPLETED

05:00
06:00
07:00
08:00
09:00
10:00
11:00
12:00
1:00
2:00
3:00
4:00
5:00
6:00
7:00
8:00
9:00

WATER:
○ ○ ○ ○
○ ○ ○ ○

GOALS:

HOME:

SELF:

WORK:

TO DO:
- [ ]
- [ ]
- [ ]
- [ ]
- [ ]
- [ ]
- [ ]
- [ ]
- [ ]
- [ ]
- [ ]
- [ ]
- [ ]
- [ ]
- [ ]
- [ ]
- [ ]

LAY DOWN YOUR *Sins*

LIFT UP YOUR *Wins*

- [ ] PRAY FOR TODAY, HIS COVERING AS YOU SLEEP, AND HIS PRESENCE TOMORROW
- [ ] MOVE UNDONE TO-DO'S TO TOMORROW

Journal
RECORD NUDGES FROM DAILY DEVOTION

The Legacy Leaders like to use a popular process of P.R.A.Y. (pause, rejoice, ask, yield) after their daily Devo. As things come to you trust that it is the Holy Spirit nudging you and then do PROBLEM/WORD/GIFT/CHOICE to tap into God's help.

FREE JOURNALING OF WHATEVER IS ON YOUR MIND AS YOU THINK, LISTEN, OR WHAT WEIGHS ON YOUR MIND:

....
....
....

P (PAUSE)
....

R (REJOICE)
....

A (ASK)
....

Y (YIELD)
....
....

WAS THERE ANYTHING YOU FELT NUDGED TO WORK ON? LET'S TAP INTO THE WORD FOR HELP

PROBLEM (EXAMPLES ARE WORRY, FEAR, DOUBT, INSECURITY, IMPATIENCE)
....

WORD (GO TO THE INTERNET & LOOK UP 'MEMORY VERSES ON YOUR TOPIC & RECORD A FEW HERE)
....
....
....

GIFT (WRITE ABOUT WHAT LIFE WOULD LIKE BE IF YOU FOLLOW THE WORD)
....
....

CHOICE (YOU HAVE FREE WILL, WRITE OUT HOW YOU PLAN TO FOLLOW THROUGH)
....

MEDITATION *Verse*

(REWRITE YESTERDAY'S PROBLEM-WORD-GIFT-CHOICE MEMORY VERSE HERE

Date: _____

| S | M | T | W | T | F | S |

MEALS:

BREAKFAST

LUNCH

DINNER

PRIORITIES:

☐ EXERCISED
☐ DEVOTIONS & JOURNAL COMPLETED

05:00
06:00
07:00
08:00
09:00
10:00
11:00
12:00
1:00
2:00
3:00
4:00
5:00
6:00
7:00
8:00
9:00

☐ PRAY FOR TODAY, HIS COVERING AS YOU SLEEP, AND HIS PRESENCE TOMORROW
☐ MOVE UNDONE TO-DO'S TO TOMORROW

WATER:
○ ○ ○ ○
○ ○ ○ ○

GOALS:

HOME:

SELF:

WORK:

TO DO:
☐
☐
☐
☐
☐
☐
☐
☐
☐
☐
☐
☐
☐
☐
☐
☐
☐

LAY DOWN YOUR *Sins*

LIFT UP YOUR *Wins*

Journal
RECORD NUDGES FROM DAILY DEVOTION

The Legacy Leaders like to use a popular process of P.R.A.Y. (pause, rejoice, ask, yield) after their daily Devo. As things come to you trust that it is the Holy Spirit nudging you and then do PROBLEM/WORD/GIFT/CHOICE to tap into God's help.

FREE JOURNALING OF WHATEVER IS ON YOUR MIND AS YOU THINK, LISTEN, OR WHAT WEIGHS ON YOUR MIND:

....
....
....

P (PAUSE)
....

R (REJOICE)
....

A (ASK)
....

Y (YIELD)
....

WAS THERE ANYTHING YOU FELT NUDGED TO WORK ON? LET'S TAP INTO THE WORD FOR HELP

PROBLEM (EXAMPLES ARE WORRY, FEAR, DOUBT, INSECURITY, IMPATIENCE)
....

WORD (GO TO THE INTERNET & LOOK UP 'MEMORY VERSES ON YOUR TOPIC & RECORD A FEW HERE)
....
....
....

GIFT (WRITE ABOUT WHAT LIFE WOULD LIKE BE IF YOU FOLLOW THE WORD)
....

CHOICE (YOU HAVE FREE WILL, WRITE OUT HOW YOU PLAN TO FOLLOW THROUGH)
....

MEDITATION *Verse*

(REWRITE YESTERDAY'S PROBLEM-WORD-GIFT-CHOICE MEMORY VERSE HERE)

Date:_____

| S | M | T | W | T | F | S |

MEALS:

BREAKFAST

LUNCH

DINNER

PRIORITIES:

- [ ] EXERCISED
- [ ] DEVOTIONS & JOURNAL COMPLETED

05:00
06:00
07:00
08:00
09:00
10:00
11:00
12:00
1:00
2:00
3:00
4:00
5:00
6:00
7:00
8:00
9:00

- [ ] PRAY FOR TODAY, HIS COVERING AS YOU SLEEP, AND HIS PRESENCE TOMORROW
- [ ] MOVE UNDONE TO-DO'S TO TOMORROW

WATER:
○ ○ ○ ○
○ ○ ○ ○

GOALS:

HOME:

SELF:

WORK:

TO DO:

LAY DOWN YOUR *Sins*

LIFT UP YOUR *Wins*

Journal
RECORD NUDGES FROM DAILY DEVOTION

The Legacy Leaders like to use a popular process of P.R.A.Y. (pause, rejoice, ask, yield) after their daily Devo. As things come to you trust that it is the Holy Spirit nudging you and then do PROBLEM/WORD/GIFT/CHOICE to tap into God's help.

FREE JOURNALING OF WHATEVER IS ON YOUR MIND AS YOU THINK, LISTEN, OR WHAT WEIGHS ON YOUR MIND:

....
....
....

P (PAUSE)
....

R (REJOICE)
....

A (ASK)
....

Y (YIELD)
....

WAS THERE ANYTHING YOU FELT NUDGED TO WORK ON? LET'S TAP INTO THE WORD FOR HELP

PROBLEM (EXAMPLES ARE WORRY, FEAR, DOUBT, INSECURITY, IMPATIENCE)
....

WORD (GO TO THE INTERNET & LOOK UP 'MEMORY VERSES ON YOUR TOPIC & RECORD A FEW HERE)
....
....
....

GIFT (WRITE ABOUT WHAT LIFE WOULD LIKE BE IF YOU FOLLOW THE WORD)
....

CHOICE (YOU HAVE FREE WILL, WRITE OUT HOW YOU PLAN TO FOLLOW THROUGH)
....

MEDITATION *Verse*

(REWRITE YESTERDAY'S PROBLEM-WORD-GIFT-CHOICE MEMORY VERSE HERE

Date: _____

| S | M | T | W | T | F | S |

MEALS:
BREAKFAST

LUNCH

DINNER

PRIORITIES:
- [ ] EXERCISED
- [ ] DEVOTIONS & JOURNAL COMPLETED

05:00
06:00
07:00
08:00
09:00
10:00
11:00
12:00
1:00
2:00
3:00
4:00
5:00
6:00
7:00
8:00
9:00

WATER:
○ ○ ○ ○
○ ○ ○ ○

GOALS:

HOME:

SELF:

WORK:

TO DO:
- [ ]
- [ ]
- [ ]
- [ ]
- [ ]
- [ ]
- [ ]
- [ ]
- [ ]
- [ ]
- [ ]
- [ ]
- [ ]
- [ ]
- [ ]

LAY DOWN YOUR *Sins*

LIFT UP YOUR *Wins*

- [ ] PRAY FOR TODAY, HIS COVERING AS YOU SLEEP, AND HIS PRESENCE TOMORROW
- [ ] MOVE UNDONE TO-DO'S TO TOMORROW

Journal
RECORD NUDGES FROM DAILY DEVOTION

The Legacy Leaders like to use a popular process of P.R.A.Y. (pause, rejoice, ask, yield) after their daily Devo. As things come to you trust that it is the Holy Spirit nudging you and then do PROBLEM/WORD/GIFT/CHOICE to tap into God's help.

FREE JOURNALING OF WHATEVER IS ON YOUR MIND AS YOU THINK, LISTEN, OR WHAT WEIGHS ON YOUR MIND:

....
....
....

P (PAUSE)
....

R (REJOICE)
....

A (ASK)
....

Y (YIELD)
....
....

WAS THERE ANYTHING YOU FELT NUDGED TO WORK ON? LET'S TAP INTO THE WORD FOR HELP

PROBLEM (EXAMPLES ARE WORRY, FEAR, DOUBT, INSECURITY, IMPATIENCE)
....

WORD (GO TO THE INTERNET & LOOK UP 'MEMORY VERSES ON YOUR TOPIC & RECORD A FEW HERE)
....
....
....

GIFT (WRITE ABOUT WHAT LIFE WOULD LIKE BE IF YOU FOLLOW THE WORD)
....

CHOICE (YOU HAVE FREE WILL, WRITE OUT HOW YOU PLAN TO FOLLOW THROUGH)
....

MEDITATION *Verse*

(REWRITE YESTERDAY'S PROBLEM-WORD-GIFT-CHOICE MEMORY VERSE HERE

Date: _____

| S | M | T | W | T | F | S |

MEALS:

BREAKFAST

LUNCH

DINNER

PRIORITIES:

☐ EXERCISED
☐ DEVOTIONS & JOURNAL COMPLETED

05:00
06:00
07:00
08:00
09:00
10:00
11:00
12:00
1:00
2:00
3:00
4:00
5:00
6:00
7:00
8:00
9:00

WATER:
○ ○ ○ ○
○ ○ ○ ○

GOALS:

HOME:

SELF:

WORK:

TO DO:
☐
☐
☐
☐
☐
☐
☐
☐
☐
☐
☐
☐
☐
☐
☐
☐
☐

LAY DOWN YOUR *Sins*

LIFT UP YOUR *Wins*

☐ PRAY FOR TODAY, HIS COVERING AS YOU SLEEP, AND HIS PRESENCE TOMORROW
☐ MOVE UNDONE TO-DO'S TO TOMORROW

Journal
RECORD NUDGES FROM DAILY DEVOTION

The Legacy Leaders like to use a popular process of P.R.A.Y. (pause, rejoice, ask, yield) after their daily Devo. As things come to you trust that it is the Holy Spirit nudging you and then do PROBLEM/WORD/GIFT/CHOICE to tap into God's help.

FREE JOURNALING OF WHATEVER IS ON YOUR MIND AS YOU THINK, LISTEN, OR WHAT WEIGHS ON YOUR MIND:

P (PAUSE)

R (REJOICE)

A (ASK)

Y (YIELD)

WAS THERE ANYTHING YOU FELT NUDGED TO WORK ON? LET'S TAP INTO THE WORD FOR HELP

PROBLEM (EXAMPLES ARE WORRY, FEAR, DOUBT, INSECURITY, IMPATIENCE)

WORD (GO TO THE INTERNET & LOOK UP 'MEMORY VERSES ON YOUR TOPIC & RECORD A FEW HERE)

GIFT (WRITE ABOUT WHAT LIFE WOULD LIKE BE IF YOU FOLLOW THE WORD)

CHOICE (YOU HAVE FREE WILL, WRITE OUT HOW YOU PLAN TO FOLLOW THROUGH)

MEDITATION *Verse*

Date: _____

| S | M | T | W | T | F | S |

(REWRITE YESTERDAY'S PROBLEM-WORD-GIFT-CHOICE MEMORY VERSE HERE)

MEALS:

BREAKFAST

LUNCH

DINNER

PRIORITIES:

☐ EXERCISED
☐ DEVOTIONS & JOURNAL COMPLETED

05:00
06:00
07:00
08:00
09:00
10:00
11:00
12:00
1:00
2:00
3:00
4:00
5:00
6:00
7:00
8:00
9:00

WATER:
○ ○ ○ ○
○ ○ ○ ○

GOALS:

HOME:

SELF:

WORK:

TO DO:
☐
☐
☐
☐
☐
☐
☐
☐
☐
☐
☐
☐
☐
☐

LAY DOWN YOUR *Sins*

LIFT UP YOUR *Wins*

☐ PRAY FOR TODAY, HIS COVERING AS YOU SLEEP, AND HIS PRESENCE TOMORROW
☐ MOVE UNDONE TO-DO'S TO TOMORROW

Journal
RECORD NUDGES FROM DAILY DEVOTION

The Legacy Leaders like to use a popular process of P.R.A.Y. (pause, rejoice, ask, yield) after their daily Devo. As things come to you trust that it is the Holy Spirit nudging you and then do PROBLEM/WORD/GIFT/CHOICE to tap into God's help.

FREE JOURNALING OF WHATEVER IS ON YOUR MIND AS YOU THINK, LISTEN, OR WHAT WEIGHS ON YOUR MIND:
....
....
....

P (PAUSE)
....

R (REJOICE)
....

A (ASK)
....

Y (YIELD)
....
....

WAS THERE ANYTHING YOU FELT NUDGED TO WORK ON? LET'S TAP INTO THE WORD FOR HELP

PROBLEM (EXAMPLES ARE WORRY, FEAR, DOUBT, INSECURITY, IMPATIENCE)
....

WORD (GO TO THE INTERNET & LOOK UP 'MEMORY VERSES ON YOUR TOPIC & RECORD A FEW HERE)
....
....
....

GIFT (WRITE ABOUT WHAT LIFE WOULD LIKE BE IF YOU FOLLOW THE WORD)
....

CHOICE (YOU HAVE FREE WILL. WRITE OUT HOW YOU PLAN TO FOLLOW THROUGH)
....
....

MEDITATION *Verse*

(REWRITE YESTERDAY'S PROBLEM-WORD-GIFT-CHOICE MEMORY VERSE HERE)

Date: _____

| S | M | T | W | T | F | S |

MEALS:

BREAKFAST

LUNCH

DINNER

PRIORITIES:

☐ EXERCISED
☐ DEVOTIONS & JOURNAL COMPLETED

05:00
06:00
07:00
08:00
09:00
10:00
11:00
12:00
1:00
2:00
3:00
4:00
5:00
6:00
7:00
8:00
9:00

WATER:
○ ○ ○ ○
○ ○ ○ ○

GOALS:

HOME:

SELF:

WORK:

TO DO:

☐
☐
☐
☐
☐
☐
☐
☐
☐
☐
☐
☐

LAY DOWN YOUR *Sins*

LIFT UP YOUR *Wins*

☐ PRAY FOR TODAY, HIS COVERING AS YOU SLEEP, AND HIS PRESENCE TOMORROW
☐ MOVE UNDONE TO-DO'S TO TOMORROW

Journal
RECORD NUDGES FROM DAILY DEVOTION

The Legacy Leaders like to use a popular process of P.R.A.Y. (pause, rejoice, ask, yield) after their daily Devo. As things come to you trust that it is the Holy Spirit nudging you and then do PROBLEM/WORD/GIFT/CHOICE to tap into God's help.

<u>FREE JOURNALING OF WHATEVER IS ON YOUR MIND AS YOU THINK, LISTEN, OR WHAT WEIGHS ON YOUR MIND:</u>

P (PAUSE)

R (REJOICE)

A (ASK)

Y (YIELD)

<u>WAS THERE ANYTHING YOU FELT NUDGED TO WORK ON? LET'S TAP INTO THE WORD FOR HELP</u>

PROBLEM (EXAMPLES ARE WORRY, FEAR, DOUBT, INSECURITY, IMPATIENCE)

WORD (GO TO THE INTERNET & LOOK UP 'MEMORY VERSES ON YOUR TOPIC & RECORD A FEW HERE)

GIFT (WRITE ABOUT WHAT LIFE WOULD LIKE BE IF YOU FOLLOW THE WORD)

CHOICE (YOU HAVE FREE WILL, WRITE OUT HOW YOU PLAN TO FOLLOW THROUGH)

MEDITATION *Verse*

Date:_____

| S | M | T | W | T | F | S |

(REWRITE YESTERDAY'S PROBLEM-WORD-GIFT-CHOICE MEMORY VERSE HERE)

MEALS:

BREAKFAST

LUNCH

DINNER

PRIORITIES:

☐ EXERCISED
☐ DEVOTIONS & JOURNAL COMPLETED

05:00
06:00
07:00
08:00
09:00
10:00
11:00
12:00
1:00
2:00
3:00
4:00
5:00
6:00
7:00
8:00
9:00

☐ PRAY FOR TODAY, HIS COVERING AS YOU SLEEP, AND HIS PRESENCE TOMORROW
☐ MOVE UNDONE TO-DO'S TO TOMORROW

WATER:
○ ○ ○ ○
○ ○ ○ ○

GOALS:

HOME:

SELF:

WORK:

TO DO:

☐
☐
☐
☐
☐
☐
☐
☐
☐
☐
☐
☐
☐
☐
☐

LAY DOWN YOUR *Sins*

LIFT UP YOUR *Wins*

Journal
RECORD NUDGES FROM DAILY DEVOTION

The Legacy Leaders like to use a popular process of P.R.A.Y. (pause, rejoice, ask, yield) after their daily Devo. As things come to you trust that it is the Holy Spirit nudging you and then do PROBLEM/WORD/GIFT/CHOICE to tap into God's help.

FREE JOURNALING OF WHATEVER IS ON YOUR MIND AS YOU THINK, LISTEN, OR WHAT WEIGHS ON YOUR MIND:
....
....
....

P (PAUSE)
....

R (REJOICE)
....

A (ASK)
....

Y (YIELD)
....
....

WAS THERE ANYTHING YOU FELT NUDGED TO WORK ON? LET'S TAP INTO THE WORD FOR HELP

PROBLEM (EXAMPLES ARE WORRY, FEAR, DOUBT, INSECURITY, IMPATIENCE)
....

WORD (GO TO THE INTERNET & LOOK UP 'MEMORY VERSES ON YOUR TOPIC & RECORD A FEW HERE)
....
....
....

GIFT (WRITE ABOUT WHAT LIFE WOULD LIKE BE IF YOU FOLLOW THE WORD)
....

CHOICE (YOU HAVE FREE WILL, WRITE OUT HOW YOU PLAN TO FOLLOW THROUGH)
....

MEDITATION *Verse*

Date:_____

| S | M | T | W | T | F | S |

(REWRITE YESTERDAY'S PROBLEM-WORD-GIFT-CHOICE MEMORY VERSE HERE)

MEALS:

BREAKFAST

LUNCH

DINNER

PRIORITIES:

☐ EXERCISED
☐ DEVOTIONS & JOURNAL COMPLETED

05:00
06:00
07:00
08:00
09:00
10:00
11:00
12:00
1:00
2:00
3:00
4:00
5:00
6:00
7:00
8:00
9:00

☐ PRAY FOR TODAY, HIS COVERING AS YOU SLEEP, AND HIS PRESENCE TOMORROW
☐ MOVE UNDONE TO-DO'S TO TOMORROW

WATER:
○ ○ ○ ○
○ ○ ○ ○

GOALS:

HOME:

SELF:

WORK:

TO DO:
☐
☐
☐
☐
☐
☐
☐
☐
☐
☐
☐
☐
☐
☐
☐
☐
☐

LAY DOWN YOUR *Sins*

LIFT UP YOUR *Wins*

Journal
RECORD NUDGES FROM DAILY DEVOTION

The Legacy Leaders like to use a popular process of P.R.A.Y. (pause, rejoice, ask, yield) after their daily Devo. As things come to you trust that it is the Holy Spirit nudging you and then do PROBLEM/WORD/GIFT/CHOICE to tap into God's help.

<u>FREE JOURNALING OF WHATEVER IS ON YOUR MIND AS YOU THINK, LISTEN, OR WHAT WEIGHS ON YOUR MIND:</u>

....
....
....

P (PAUSE)
....

R (REJOICE)
....

A (ASK)
....

Y (YIELD)
....
....

<u>WAS THERE ANYTHING YOU FELT NUDGED TO WORK ON? LET'S TAP INTO THE WORD FOR HELP</u>

PROBLEM (EXAMPLES ARE WORRY, FEAR, DOUBT, INSECURITY, IMPATIENCE)
....

WORD (GO TO THE INTERNET & LOOK UP 'MEMORY VERSES ON YOUR TOPIC & RECORD A FEW HERE)
....
....
....

GIFT (WRITE ABOUT WHAT LIFE WOULD LIKE BE IF YOU FOLLOW THE WORD)
....

CHOICE (YOU HAVE FREE WILL, WRITE OUT HOW YOU PLAN TO FOLLOW THROUGH)
....
....

MEDITATION *Verse*

(REWRITE YESTERDAY'S PROBLEM-WORD-GIFT-CHOICE MEMORY VERSE HERE)

Date:_____
S | M | T | W | T | F | S

MEALS:

BREAKFAST

LUNCH

DINNER

PRIORITIES:
- [ ] EXERCISED
- [ ] DEVOTIONS & JOURNAL COMPLETED

05:00
06:00
07:00
08:00
09:00
10:00
11:00
12:00
1:00
2:00
3:00
4:00
5:00
6:00
7:00
8:00
9:00

WATER:
○ ○ ○ ○
○ ○ ○ ○

GOALS:

HOME:

SELF:

WORK:

TO DO:
- [ ]
- [ ]
- [ ]
- [ ]
- [ ]
- [ ]
- [ ]
- [ ]
- [ ]
- [ ]
- [ ]
- [ ]
- [ ]
- [ ]
- [ ]

LAY DOWN YOUR *Sins*

LIFT UP YOUR *Wins*

- [ ] PRAY FOR TODAY, HIS COVERING AS YOU SLEEP, AND HIS PRESENCE TOMORROW
- [ ] MOVE UNDONE TO-DO'S TO TOMORROW

Journal
RECORD NUDGES FROM DAILY DEVOTION

The Legacy Leaders like to use a popular process of P.R.A.Y. (pause, rejoice, ask, yield) after their daily Devo. As things come to you trust that it is the Holy Spirit nudging you and then do PROBLEM/WORD/GIFT/CHOICE to tap into God's help.

FREE JOURNALING OF WHATEVER IS ON YOUR MIND AS YOU THINK, LISTEN, OR WHAT WEIGHS ON YOUR MIND:

....
....
....

P (PAUSE)
....

R (REJOICE)
....

A (ASK)
....

Y (YIELD)
....
....

WAS THERE ANYTHING YOU FELT NUDGED TO WORK ON? LET'S TAP INTO THE WORD FOR HELP

PROBLEM (EXAMPLES ARE WORRY, FEAR, DOUBT, INSECURITY, IMPATIENCE)
....

WORD (GO TO THE INTERNET & LOOK UP 'MEMORY VERSES ON YOUR TOPIC & RECORD A FEW HERE)
....
....
....

GIFT (WRITE ABOUT WHAT LIFE WOULD LIKE BE IF YOU FOLLOW THE WORD)
....

CHOICE (YOU HAVE FREE WILL, WRITE OUT HOW YOU PLAN TO FOLLOW THROUGH)
....

MEDITATION *Verse*

(REWRITE YESTERDAY'S PROBLEM-WORD-GIFT-CHOICE MEMORY VERSE HERE)

Date: _____

| S | M | T | W | T | F | S |

MEALS:

BREAKFAST

LUNCH

DINNER

PRIORITIES:

- [ ] EXERCISED
- [ ] DEVOTIONS & JOURNAL COMPLETED

05:00
06:00
07:00
08:00
09:00
10:00
11:00
12:00
1:00
2:00
3:00
4:00
5:00
6:00
7:00
8:00
9:00

WATER:
○ ○ ○ ○
○ ○ ○ ○

GOALS:

HOME:

SELF:

WORK:

TO DO:
- [ ]
- [ ]
- [ ]
- [ ]
- [ ]
- [ ]
- [ ]
- [ ]
- [ ]
- [ ]
- [ ]
- [ ]
- [ ]
- [ ]
- [ ]
- [ ]
- [ ]

LAY DOWN YOUR *Sins*

LIFT UP YOUR *Wins*

- [ ] PRAY FOR TODAY, HIS COVERING AS YOU SLEEP, AND HIS PRESENCE TOMORROW
- [ ] MOVE UNDONE TO-DO'S TO TOMORROW

Journal
RECORD NUDGES FROM DAILY DEVOTION

The Legacy Leaders like to use a popular process of P.R.A.Y. (pause, rejoice, ask, yield) after their daily Devo. As things come to you trust that it is the Holy Spirit nudging you and then do PROBLEM/WORD/GIFT/CHOICE to tap into God's help.

FREE JOURNALING OF WHATEVER IS ON YOUR MIND AS YOU THINK, LISTEN, OR WHAT WEIGHS ON YOUR MIND:

....
....
....

P (PAUSE)
....

R (REJOICE)
....

A (ASK)
....

Y (YIELD)
....
....

WAS THERE ANYTHING YOU FELT NUDGED TO WORK ON? LET'S TAP INTO THE WORD FOR HELP

PROBLEM (EXAMPLES ARE WORRY, FEAR, DOUBT, INSECURITY, IMPATIENCE)
....

WORD (GO TO THE INTERNET & LOOK UP 'MEMORY VERSES ON YOUR TOPIC & RECORD A FEW HERE)
....
....
....

GIFT (WRITE ABOUT WHAT LIFE WOULD LIKE BE IF YOU FOLLOW THE WORD)
....

CHOICE (YOU HAVE FREE WILL, WRITE OUT HOW YOU PLAN TO FOLLOW THROUGH)
....

MEDITATION *Verse*

(REWRITE YESTERDAY'S PROBLEM-WORD-GIFT-CHOICE MEMORY VERSE HERE)

Date:_____

| S | M | T | W | T | F | S |

MEALS:

BREAKFAST

LUNCH

DINNER

PRIORITIES:

- [ ] EXERCISED
- [ ] DEVOTIONS & JOURNAL COMPLETED

05:00

06:00

07:00

08:00

09:00

10:00

11:00

12:00

1:00

2:00

3:00

4:00

5:00

6:00

7:00

8:00

9:00

- [ ] PRAY FOR TODAY, HIS COVERING AS YOU SLEEP, AND HIS PRESENCE TOMORROW
- [ ] MOVE UNDONE TO-DO'S TO TOMORROW

WATER:
○ ○ ○ ○
○ ○ ○ ○

GOALS:

HOME:

SELF:

WORK:

TO DO:

- [ ]
- [ ]
- [ ]
- [ ]
- [ ]
- [ ]
- [ ]
- [ ]
- [ ]
- [ ]
- [ ]
- [ ]
- [ ]
- [ ]
- [ ]
- [ ]
- [ ]

LAY DOWN YOUR *Sins*

LIFT UP YOUR *Wins*

Journal
RECORD NUDGES FROM DAILY DEVOTION

The Legacy Leaders like to use a popular process of P.R.A.Y. (pause, rejoice, ask, yield) after their daily Devo. As things come to you trust that it is the Holy Spirit nudging you and then do PROBLEM/WORD/GIFT/CHOICE to tap into God's help.

FREE JOURNALING OF WHATEVER IS ON YOUR MIND AS YOU THINK, LISTEN, OR WHAT WEIGHS ON YOUR MIND:

....
....
....

P (PAUSE)
....

R (REJOICE)
....

A (ASK)
....

Y (YIELD)
....

WAS THERE ANYTHING YOU FELT NUDGED TO WORK ON? LET'S TAP INTO THE WORD FOR HELP

PROBLEM (EXAMPLES ARE WORRY, FEAR, DOUBT, INSECURITY, IMPATIENCE)
....

WORD (GO TO THE INTERNET & LOOK UP 'MEMORY VERSES ON YOUR TOPIC & RECORD A FEW HERE)
....
....

GIFT (WRITE ABOUT WHAT LIFE WOULD LIKE BE IF YOU FOLLOW THE WORD)
....

CHOICE (YOU HAVE FREE WILL, WRITE OUT HOW YOU PLAN TO FOLLOW THROUGH)
....

MEDITATION *Verse*

(REWRITE YESTERDAY'S PROBLEM-WORD-GIFT-CHOICE MEMORY VERSE HERE)

Date: _____

S	M	T	W	T	F	S

MEALS:

BREAKFAST

LUNCH

DINNER

PRIORITIES:

- [ ] EXERCISED
- [ ] DEVOTIONS & JOURNAL COMPLETED

05:00
06:00
07:00
08:00
09:00
10:00
11:00
12:00
1:00
2:00
3:00
4:00
5:00
6:00
7:00
8:00
9:00

WATER:
○ ○ ○ ○
○ ○ ○ ○

GOALS:

HOME:

SELF:

WORK:

TO DO:
- [ ]
- [ ]
- [ ]
- [ ]
- [ ]
- [ ]
- [ ]
- [ ]
- [ ]
- [ ]
- [ ]
- [ ]
- [ ]
- [ ]

LAY DOWN YOUR *Sins*

LIFT UP YOUR *Wins*

- [ ] PRAY FOR TODAY, HIS COVERING AS YOU SLEEP, AND HIS PRESENCE TOMORROW
- [ ] MOVE UNDONE TO-DO'S TO TOMORROW

Journal
RECORD NUDGES FROM DAILY DEVOTION

The Legacy Leaders like to use a popular process of P.R.A.Y. (pause, rejoice, ask, yield) after their daily Devo. As things come to you trust that it is the Holy Spirit nudging you and then do PROBLEM/WORD/GIFT/CHOICE to tap into God's help.

FREE JOURNALING OF WHATEVER IS ON YOUR MIND AS YOU THINK, LISTEN, OR WHAT WEIGHS ON YOUR MIND:

....
....
....

P (PAUSE)
....

R (REJOICE)
....

A (ASK)
....

Y (YIELD)
....
....

WAS THERE ANYTHING YOU FELT NUDGED TO WORK ON? LET'S TAP INTO THE WORD FOR HELP

PROBLEM (EXAMPLES ARE WORRY, FEAR, DOUBT, INSECURITY, IMPATIENCE)
....

WORD (GO TO THE INTERNET & LOOK UP 'MEMORY VERSES ON YOUR TOPIC & RECORD A FEW HERE)
....
....
....

GIFT (WRITE ABOUT WHAT LIFE WOULD LIKE BE IF YOU FOLLOW THE WORD)
....

CHOICE (YOU HAVE FREE WILL, WRITE OUT HOW YOU PLAN TO FOLLOW THROUGH)
....

Notes

Notes

Month

SUN	MON	TUE	WED	THU	FRI	SAT

BIRTHDAYS/ANNIVERSARIES

_____
_____

FUTURE EVENTS TO CARRY OVER

_____
_____

FULFILL YOUR LEGACY | NICCIEKLIEGL.COM | LIFE & BUSINESS COACH

FULFILL YOUR LEGACY

Budget

MONTHLY BALANCE GOAL: _____

INCOME

DATE	SOURCE	CATEGORY	AMOUNT

BILLS & FIXED EXPENSES

DATE	SOURCE	AMOUNT

VARIABLE EXPENSES

DATE	SOURCE	AMOUNT

SUMMARY

SOURCE	AMOUNT
INCOME	
BILLS & FIXED EXPENSES	
VARIABLE EXPENSES	
BALANCE	

FULFILL YOUR LEGACY | NICCIEKLIEGL.COM | LIFE & BUSINESS COACH

FULFILL YOUR LEGACY

MEDITATION *Verse*

(REWRITE YESTERDAY'S PROBLEM-WORD-GIFT-CHOICE MEMORY VERSE HERE)

Date: _____

| S | M | T | W | T | F | S |

MEALS:

BREAKFAST

LUNCH

DINNER

PRIORITIES:

☐ EXERCISED
☐ DEVOTIONS & JOURNAL COMPLETED

05:00
06:00
07:00
08:00
09:00
10:00
11:00
12:00
1:00
2:00
3:00
4:00
5:00
6:00
7:00
8:00
9:00

WATER:
○ ○ ○ ○
○ ○ ○ ○

GOALS:

HOME:

SELF:

WORK:

TO DO:
☐
☐
☐
☐
☐
☐
☐
☐
☐
☐
☐
☐
☐
☐

LAY DOWN YOUR *Sins*

LIFT UP YOUR *Wins*

☐ PRAY FOR TODAY, HIS COVERING AS YOU SLEEP, AND HIS PRESENCE TOMORROW
☐ MOVE UNDONE TO-DO'S TO TOMORROW

Journal
RECORD NUDGES FROM DAILY DEVOTION

The Legacy Leaders like to use a popular process of P.R.A.Y. (pause, rejoice, ask, yield) after their daily Devo. As things come to you trust that it is the Holy Spirit nudging you and then do PROBLEM/WORD/GIFT/CHOICE to tap into God's help.

FREE JOURNALING OF WHATEVER IS ON YOUR MIND AS YOU THINK, LISTEN, OR WHAT WEIGHS ON YOUR MIND:

....
....
....

P (PAUSE)
....

R (REJOICE)
....

A (ASK)
....

Y (YIELD)
....
....

WAS THERE ANYTHING YOU FELT NUDGED TO WORK ON? LET'S TAP INTO THE WORD FOR HELP

PROBLEM (EXAMPLES ARE WORRY, FEAR, DOUBT, INSECURITY, IMPATIENCE)
....

WORD (GO TO THE INTERNET & LOOK UP 'MEMORY VERSES ON YOUR TOPIC & RECORD A FEW HERE)
....
....
....

GIFT (WRITE ABOUT WHAT LIFE WOULD LIKE BE IF YOU FOLLOW THE WORD)
....

CHOICE (YOU HAVE FREE WILL, WRITE OUT HOW YOU PLAN TO FOLLOW THROUGH)
....

MEDITATION *Verse*

(REWRITE YESTERDAY'S PROBLEM-WORD-GIFT-CHOICE MEMORY VERSE HERE)

Date: _____

| S | M | T | W | T | F | S |

MEALS:

BREAKFAST

LUNCH

DINNER

PRIORITIES:

☐ EXERCISED
☐ DEVOTIONS & JOURNAL COMPLETED

05:00
06:00
07:00
08:00
09:00
10:00
11:00
12:00
1:00
2:00
3:00
4:00
5:00
6:00
7:00
8:00
9:00

WATER:
○ ○ ○ ○
○ ○ ○ ○

GOALS:

HOME:

SELF:

WORK:

TO DO:
☐
☐
☐
☐
☐
☐
☐
☐
☐
☐
☐
☐
☐
☐
☐
☐

LAY DOWN YOUR *Sins*

LIFT UP YOUR *Wins*

☐ PRAY FOR TODAY, HIS COVERING AS YOU SLEEP, AND HIS PRESENCE TOMORROW
☐ MOVE UNDONE TO-DO'S TO TOMORROW

Journal
RECORD NUDGES FROM DAILY DEVOTION

The Legacy Leaders like to use a popular process of P.R.A.Y. (pause, rejoice, ask, yield) after their daily Devo. As things come to you trust that it is the Holy Spirit nudging you and then do PROBLEM/WORD/GIFT/CHOICE to tap into God's help.

FREE JOURNALING OF WHATEVER IS ON YOUR MIND AS YOU THINK, LISTEN, OR WHAT WEIGHS ON YOUR MIND:

....
....
....

P (PAUSE)
....

R (REJOICE)
....

A (ASK)
....

Y (YIELD)
....
....

WAS THERE ANYTHING YOU FELT NUDGED TO WORK ON? LET'S TAP INTO THE WORD FOR HELP

PROBLEM (EXAMPLES ARE WORRY, FEAR, DOUBT, INSECURITY, IMPATIENCE)
....

WORD (GO TO THE INTERNET & LOOK UP 'MEMORY VERSES ON YOUR TOPIC & RECORD A FEW HERE)
....
....
....

GIFT (WRITE ABOUT WHAT LIFE WOULD LIKE BE IF YOU FOLLOW THE WORD)
....

CHOICE (YOU HAVE FREE WILL. WRITE OUT HOW YOU PLAN TO FOLLOW THROUGH)
....

MEDITATION *Verse*

(REWRITE YESTERDAY'S PROBLEM-WORD-GIFT-CHOICE MEMORY VERSE HERE)

Date: _____

| S | M | T | W | T | F | S |

MEALS:

BREAKFAST

LUNCH

DINNER

PRIORITIES:

☐ EXERCISED
☐ DEVOTIONS & JOURNAL COMPLETED

- 05:00
- 06:00
- 07:00
- 08:00
- 09:00
- 10:00
- 11:00
- 12:00
- 1:00
- 2:00
- 3:00
- 4:00
- 5:00
- 6:00
- 7:00
- 8:00
- 9:00

☐ PRAY FOR TODAY, HIS COVERING AS YOU SLEEP, AND HIS PRESENCE TOMORROW
☐ MOVE UNDONE TO-DO'S TO TOMORROW

WATER:
○ ○ ○ ○
○ ○ ○ ○

GOALS:

HOME:

SELF:

WORK:

TO DO:
☐
☐
☐
☐
☐
☐
☐
☐
☐
☐
☐
☐
☐

LAY DOWN YOUR *Sins*

LIFT UP YOUR *Wins*

Journal
RECORD NUDGES FROM DAILY DEVOTION

The Legacy Leaders like to use a popular process of P.R.A.Y. (pause, rejoice, ask, yield) after their daily Devo. As things come to you trust that it is the Holy Spirit nudging you and then do PROBLEM/WORD/GIFT/CHOICE to tap into God's help.

FREE JOURNALING OF WHATEVER IS ON YOUR MIND AS YOU THINK, LISTEN, OR WHAT WEIGHS ON YOUR MIND:

....
....
....
....

P (PAUSE)
....

R (REJOICE)
....

A (ASK)
....

Y (YIELD)
....
....

WAS THERE ANYTHING YOU FELT NUDGED TO WORK ON? LET'S TAP INTO THE WORD FOR HELP

PROBLEM (EXAMPLES ARE WORRY, FEAR, DOUBT, INSECURITY, IMPATIENCE)
....

WORD (GO TO THE INTERNET & LOOK UP 'MEMORY VERSES ON YOUR TOPIC & RECORD A FEW HERE)
....
....
....

GIFT (WRITE ABOUT WHAT LIFE WOULD LIKE BE IF YOU FOLLOW THE WORD)
....

CHOICE (YOU HAVE FREE WILL, WRITE OUT HOW YOU PLAN TO FOLLOW THROUGH)
....

MEDITATION *Verse*

(REWRITE YESTERDAY'S PROBLEM-WORD-GIFT-CHOICE MEMORY VERSE HERE)

Date: _____

| S | M | T | W | T | F | S |

MEALS:

BREAKFAST

LUNCH

DINNER

PRIORITIES:

- [ ] EXERCISED
- [ ] DEVOTIONS & JOURNAL COMPLETED

05:00
06:00
07:00
08:00
09:00
10:00
11:00
12:00
1:00
2:00
3:00
4:00
5:00
6:00
7:00
8:00
9:00

- [ ] PRAY FOR TODAY, HIS COVERING AS YOU SLEEP, AND HIS PRESENCE TOMORROW
- [ ] MOVE UNDONE TO-DO'S TO TOMORROW

WATER:
○ ○ ○ ○
○ ○ ○ ○

GOALS:

HOME:

SELF:

WORK:

TO DO:
- [ ]
- [ ]
- [ ]
- [ ]
- [ ]
- [ ]
- [ ]
- [ ]
- [ ]
- [ ]
- [ ]
- [ ]
- [ ]

LAY DOWN YOUR *Sins*

LIFT UP YOUR *Wins*

Journal
RECORD NUDGES FROM DAILY DEVOTION

The Legacy Leaders like to use a popular process of P.R.A.Y. (pause, rejoice, ask, yield) after their daily Devo. As things come to you trust that it is the Holy Spirit nudging you and then do PROBLEM/WORD/GIFT/CHOICE to tap into God's help.

FREE JOURNALING OF WHATEVER IS ON YOUR MIND AS YOU THINK, LISTEN, OR WHAT WEIGHS ON YOUR MIND:

....
....
....

P (PAUSE)
....

R (REJOICE)
....

A (ASK)
....

Y (YIELD)
....
....

WAS THERE ANYTHING YOU FELT NUDGED TO WORK ON? LET'S TAP INTO THE WORD FOR HELP

PROBLEM (EXAMPLES ARE WORRY, FEAR, DOUBT, INSECURITY, IMPATIENCE)
....

WORD (GO TO THE INTERNET & LOOK UP 'MEMORY VERSES ON YOUR TOPIC & RECORD A FEW HERE)
....
....
....

GIFT (WRITE ABOUT WHAT LIFE WOULD LIKE BE IF YOU FOLLOW THE WORD)
....

CHOICE (YOU HAVE FREE WILL, WRITE OUT HOW YOU PLAN TO FOLLOW THROUGH)
....

MEDITATION *Verse*

(REWRITE YESTERDAY'S PROBLEM-WORD-GIFT-CHOICE MEMORY VERSE HERE)

Date: _____

| S | M | T | W | T | F | S |

MEALS:

BREAKFAST

LUNCH

DINNER

PRIORITIES:

- [ ] EXERCISED
- [ ] DEVOTIONS & JOURNAL COMPLETED

05:00
06:00
07:00
08:00
09:00
10:00
11:00
12:00
1:00
2:00
3:00
4:00
5:00
6:00
7:00
8:00
9:00

WATER:
○ ○ ○ ○
○ ○ ○ ○

GOALS:

HOME:

SELF:

WORK:

TO DO:
- [ ]
- [ ]
- [ ]
- [ ]
- [ ]
- [ ]
- [ ]
- [ ]
- [ ]
- [ ]
- [ ]
- [ ]
- [ ]
- [ ]
- [ ]

LAY DOWN YOUR *Sins*

LIFT UP YOUR *Wins*

- [ ] PRAY FOR TODAY, HIS COVERING AS YOU SLEEP, AND HIS PRESENCE TOMORROW
- [ ] MOVE UNDONE TO-DO'S TO TOMORROW

Journal
RECORD NUDGES FROM DAILY DEVOTION

The Legacy Leaders like to use a popular process of P.R.A.Y. (pause, rejoice, ask, yield) after their daily Devo. As things come to you trust that it is the Holy Spirit nudging you and then do PROBLEM/WORD/GIFT/CHOICE to tap into God's help.

FREE JOURNALING OF WHATEVER IS ON YOUR MIND AS YOU THINK, LISTEN, OR WHAT WEIGHS ON YOUR MIND:

....
....
....

P (PAUSE)
....

R (REJOICE)
....

A (ASK)
....

Y (YIELD)
....
....

WAS THERE ANYTHING YOU FELT NUDGED TO WORK ON? LET'S TAP INTO THE WORD FOR HELP

PROBLEM (EXAMPLES ARE WORRY, FEAR, DOUBT, INSECURITY, IMPATIENCE)
....

WORD (GO TO THE INTERNET & LOOK UP 'MEMORY VERSES ON YOUR TOPIC & RECORD A FEW HERE)
....
....
....

GIFT (WRITE ABOUT WHAT LIFE WOULD LIKE BE IF YOU FOLLOW THE WORD)
....

CHOICE (YOU HAVE FREE WILL, WRITE OUT HOW YOU PLAN TO FOLLOW THROUGH)
....

MEDITATION *Verse*

(REWRITE YESTERDAY'S PROBLEM-WORD-GIFT-CHOICE MEMORY VERSE HERE)

Date: _____

| S | M | T | W | T | F | S |

MEALS:

BREAKFAST

LUNCH

DINNER

PRIORITIES:

- [ ] EXERCISED
- [ ] DEVOTIONS & JOURNAL COMPLETED

05:00
06:00
07:00
08:00
09:00
10:00
11:00
12:00
1:00
2:00
3:00
4:00
5:00
6:00
7:00
8:00
9:00

WATER:
○ ○ ○ ○
○ ○ ○ ○

GOALS:

HOME:

SELF:

WORK:

TO DO:
- [ ]
- [ ]
- [ ]
- [ ]
- [ ]
- [ ]
- [ ]
- [ ]
- [ ]
- [ ]
- [ ]
- [ ]
- [ ]
- [ ]
- [ ]
- [ ]
- [ ]

LAY DOWN YOUR *Sins*

LIFT UP YOUR *Wins*

- [ ] PRAY FOR TODAY, HIS COVERING AS YOU SLEEP, AND HIS PRESENCE TOMORROW
- [ ] MOVE UNDONE TO-DO'S TO TOMORROW

Journal
RECORD NUDGES FROM DAILY DEVOTION

The Legacy Leaders like to use a popular process of P.R.A.Y. (pause, rejoice, ask, yield) after their daily Devo. As things come to you trust that it is the Holy Spirit nudging you and then do PROBLEM/WORD/GIFT/CHOICE to tap into God's help.

FREE JOURNALING OF WHATEVER IS ON YOUR MIND AS YOU THINK, LISTEN, OR WHAT WEIGHS ON YOUR MIND:

....
....
....

P (PAUSE)
....

R (REJOICE)
....

A (ASK)
....

Y (YIELD)
....
....

WAS THERE ANYTHING YOU FELT NUDGED TO WORK ON? LET'S TAP INTO THE WORD FOR HELP

PROBLEM (EXAMPLES ARE WORRY, FEAR, DOUBT, INSECURITY, IMPATIENCE)
....

WORD (GO TO THE INTERNET & LOOK UP 'MEMORY VERSES ON YOUR TOPIC & RECORD A FEW HERE)
....
....
....

GIFT (WRITE ABOUT WHAT LIFE WOULD LIKE BE IF YOU FOLLOW THE WORD)
....

CHOICE (YOU HAVE FREE WILL, WRITE OUT HOW YOU PLAN TO FOLLOW THROUGH)
....
....

MEDITATION *Verse*

(REWRITE YESTERDAY'S PROBLEM-WORD-GIFT-CHOICE MEMORY VERSE HERE)

Date: _____

| S | M | T | W | T | F | S |

MEALS:

BREAKFAST

LUNCH

DINNER

PRIORITIES:

- [ ] EXERCISED
- [ ] DEVOTIONS & JOURNAL COMPLETED

05:00
06:00
07:00
08:00
09:00
10:00
11:00
12:00
1:00
2:00
3:00
4:00
5:00
6:00
7:00
8:00
9:00

- [ ] PRAY FOR TODAY, HIS COVERING AS YOU SLEEP, AND HIS PRESENCE TOMORROW
- [ ] MOVE UNDONE TO-DO'S TO TOMORROW

WATER:
○ ○ ○
○ ○ ○

GOALS:

HOME:

SELF:

WORK:

TO DO:

LAY DOWN YOUR *Sins*

LIFT UP YOUR *Wins*

RECORD NUDGES *Journal* FROM DAILY DEVOTION

The Legacy Leaders like to use a popular process of P.R.A.Y. (pause, rejoice, ask, yield) after their daily Devo. As things come to you trust that it is the Holy Spirit nudging you and then do PROBLEM/WORD/GIFT/CHOICE to tap into God's help.

<u>FREE JOURNALING OF WHATEVER IS ON YOUR MIND AS YOU THINK, LISTEN, OR WHAT WEIGHS ON YOUR MIND:</u>

....
....
....

P (PAUSE)
....

R (REJOICE)
....

A (ASK)
....

Y (YIELD)
....
....

<u>WAS THERE ANYTHING YOU FELT NUDGED TO WORK ON? LET'S TAP INTO THE WORD FOR HELP</u>

PROBLEM (EXAMPLES ARE WORRY, FEAR, DOUBT, INSECURITY, IMPATIENCE)
....

WORD (GO TO THE INTERNET & LOOK UP 'MEMORY VERSES ON YOUR TOPIC & RECORD A FEW HERE)
....
....

GIFT (WRITE ABOUT WHAT LIFE WOULD LIKE BE IF YOU FOLLOW THE WORD)
....

CHOICE (YOU HAVE FREE WILL, WRITE OUT HOW YOU PLAN TO FOLLOW THROUGH)
....

MEDITATION *Verse*

(REWRITE YESTERDAY'S PROBLEM-WORD-GIFT-CHOICE MEMORY VERSE HERE)

Date: _____

| S | M | T | W | T | F | S |

MEALS:

BREAKFAST

LUNCH

DINNER

PRIORITIES:

☐ EXERCISED
☐ DEVOTIONS & JOURNAL COMPLETED

05:00
06:00
07:00
08:00
09:00
10:00
11:00
12:00
1:00
2:00
3:00
4:00
5:00
6:00
7:00
8:00
9:00

WATER:
○ ○ ○
○ ○ ○

GOALS:

HOME:

SELF:

WORK:

TO DO:
☐
☐
☐
☐
☐
☐
☐
☐
☐
☐
☐
☐
☐
☐
☐
☐
☐

LAY DOWN YOUR *Sins*

LIFT UP YOUR *Wins*

☐ PRAY FOR TODAY, HIS COVERING AS YOU SLEEP, AND HIS PRESENCE TOMORROW
☐ MOVE UNDONE TO-DO'S TO TOMORROW

Journal
RECORD NUDGES FROM DAILY DEVOTION

The Legacy Leaders like to use a popular process of P.R.A.Y. (pause, rejoice, ask, yield) after their daily Devo. As things come to you trust that it is the Holy Spirit nudging you and then do PROBLEM/WORD/GIFT/CHOICE to tap into God's help.

FREE JOURNALING OF WHATEVER IS ON YOUR MIND AS YOU THINK, LISTEN, OR WHAT WEIGHS ON YOUR MIND:

....
....
....

P (PAUSE)
....

R (REJOICE)
....

A (ASK)
....

Y (YIELD)
....
....

WAS THERE ANYTHING YOU FELT NUDGED TO WORK ON? LET'S TAP INTO THE WORD FOR HELP

PROBLEM (EXAMPLES ARE WORRY, FEAR, DOUBT, INSECURITY, IMPATIENCE)
....

WORD (GO TO THE INTERNET & LOOK UP 'MEMORY VERSES ON YOUR TOPIC & RECORD A FEW HERE)
....
....
....

GIFT (WRITE ABOUT WHAT LIFE WOULD LIKE BE IF YOU FOLLOW THE WORD)
....

CHOICE (YOU HAVE FREE WILL, WRITE OUT HOW YOU PLAN TO FOLLOW THROUGH)
....

MEDITATION *Verse*

(REWRITE YESTERDAY'S PROBLEM-WORD-GIFT-CHOICE MEMORY VERSE HERE)

Date: _____

| S | M | T | W | T | F | S |

MEALS:

BREAKFAST

LUNCH

DINNER

PRIORITIES:

- [ ] EXERCISED
- [ ] DEVOTIONS & JOURNAL COMPLETED

05:00
06:00
07:00
08:00
09:00
10:00
11:00
12:00
1:00
2:00
3:00
4:00
5:00
6:00
7:00
8:00
9:00

- [ ] PRAY FOR TODAY, HIS COVERING AS YOU SLEEP, AND HIS PRESENCE TOMORROW
- [ ] MOVE UNDONE TO-DO'S TO TOMORROW

WATER:
○ ○ ○ ○
○ ○ ○ ○

GOALS:

HOME:

SELF:

WORK:

TO DO:
- [ ]
- [ ]
- [ ]
- [ ]
- [ ]
- [ ]
- [ ]
- [ ]
- [ ]
- [ ]
- [ ]
- [ ]
- [ ]
- [ ]
- [ ]
- [ ]
- [ ]

LAY DOWN YOUR *Sins*

LIFT UP YOUR *Wins*

Journal
RECORD NUDGES FROM DAILY DEVOTION

The Legacy Leaders like to use a popular process of P.R.A.Y. (pause, rejoice, ask, yield) after their daily Devo. As things come to you trust that it is the Holy Spirit nudging you and then do PROBLEM/WORD/GIFT/CHOICE to tap into God's help.

<u>FREE JOURNALING OF WHATEVER IS ON YOUR MIND AS YOU THINK, LISTEN, OR WHAT WEIGHS ON YOUR MIND:</u>

....
....
....

P (PAUSE)
....

R (REJOICE)
....

A (ASK)
....

Y (YIELD)
....
....

<u>WAS THERE ANYTHING YOU FELT NUDGED TO WORK ON? LET'S TAP INTO THE WORD FOR HELP</u>

PROBLEM (EXAMPLES ARE WORRY, FEAR, DOUBT, INSECURITY, IMPATIENCE)
....

WORD (GO TO THE INTERNET & LOOK UP 'MEMORY VERSES ON YOUR TOPIC & RECORD A FEW HERE)
....
....

GIFT (WRITE ABOUT WHAT LIFE WOULD LIKE BE IF YOU FOLLOW THE WORD)
....

CHOICE (YOU HAVE FREE WILL, WRITE OUT HOW YOU PLAN TO FOLLOW THROUGH)
....

MEDITATION *Verse*

(REWRITE YESTERDAY'S PROBLEM-WORD-GIFT-CHOICE MEMORY VERSE HERE

Date: _____

| S | M | T | W | T | F | S |

MEALS:

BREAKFAST

LUNCH

DINNER

PRIORITIES:

- [ ] EXERCISED
- [ ] DEVOTIONS & JOURNAL COMPLETED

05:00
06:00
07:00
08:00
09:00
10:00
11:00
12:00
1:00
2:00
3:00
4:00
5:00
6:00
7:00
8:00
9:00

WATER:
○ ○ ○ ○
○ ○ ○ ○

GOALS:

HOME:

SELF:

WORK:

TO DO:

LAY DOWN YOUR *Sins*

LIFT UP YOUR *Wins*

- [ ] PRAY FOR TODAY, HIS COVERING AS YOU SLEEP, AND HIS PRESENCE TOMORROW
- [ ] MOVE UNDONE TO-DO'S TO TOMORROW

Journal
RECORD NUDGES FROM DAILY DEVOTION

The Legacy Leaders like to use a popular process of P.R.A.Y. (pause, rejoice, ask, yield) after their daily Devo. As things come to you trust that it is the Holy Spirit nudging you and then do PROBLEM/WORD/GIFT/CHOICE to tap into God's help.

<u>FREE JOURNALING OF WHATEVER IS ON YOUR MIND AS YOU THINK, LISTEN, OR WHAT WEIGHS ON YOUR MIND:</u>

....
....
....

P (PAUSE)
....

R (REJOICE)
....

A (ASK)
....

Y (YIELD)
....
....

<u>WAS THERE ANYTHING YOU FELT NUDGED TO WORK ON? LET'S TAP INTO THE WORD FOR HELP</u>

PROBLEM (EXAMPLES ARE WORRY, FEAR, DOUBT, INSECURITY, IMPATIENCE)
....

WORD (GO TO THE INTERNET & LOOK UP 'MEMORY VERSES ON YOUR TOPIC & RECORD A FEW HERE)
....
....
....

GIFT (WRITE ABOUT WHAT LIFE WOULD LIKE BE IF YOU FOLLOW THE WORD)
....

CHOICE (YOU HAVE FREE WILL, WRITE OUT HOW YOU PLAN TO FOLLOW THROUGH)
....

MEDITATION *Verse*

(REWRITE YESTERDAY'S PROBLEM-WORD-GIFT-CHOICE MEMORY VERSE HERE)

Date: _____

| S | M | T | W | T | F | S |

MEALS:

BREAKFAST

LUNCH

DINNER

PRIORITIES:

☐ EXERCISED
☐ DEVOTIONS & JOURNAL COMPLETED

- 05:00
- 06:00
- 07:00
- 08:00
- 09:00
- 10:00
- 11:00
- 12:00
- 1:00
- 2:00
- 3:00
- 4:00
- 5:00
- 6:00
- 7:00
- 8:00
- 9:00

☐ PRAY FOR TODAY, HIS COVERING AS YOU SLEEP, AND HIS PRESENCE TOMORROW
☐ MOVE UNDONE TO-DO'S TO TOMORROW

WATER:
○ ○ ○ ○
○ ○ ○ ○

GOALS:

HOME:

SELF:

WORK:

TO DO:
☐
☐
☐
☐
☐
☐
☐
☐
☐
☐
☐
☐
☐
☐
☐

LAY DOWN YOUR *Sins*

LIFT UP YOUR *Wins*

Journal

RECORD NUDGES FROM DAILY DEVOTION

The Legacy Leaders like to use a popular process of P.R.A.Y. (pause, rejoice, ask, yield) after their daily Devo. As things come to you trust that it is the Holy Spirit nudging you and then do PROBLEM/WORD/GIFT/CHOICE to tap into God's help.

FREE JOURNALING OF WHATEVER IS ON YOUR MIND AS YOU THINK, LISTEN, OR WHAT WEIGHS ON YOUR MIND:

....
....
....

P (PAUSE)
....

R (REJOICE)
....

A (ASK)
....

Y (YIELD)
....
....

WAS THERE ANYTHING YOU FELT NUDGED TO WORK ON? LET'S TAP INTO THE WORD FOR HELP

PROBLEM (EXAMPLES ARE WORRY, FEAR, DOUBT, INSECURITY, IMPATIENCE)
....

WORD (GO TO THE INTERNET & LOOK UP 'MEMORY VERSES ON YOUR TOPIC & RECORD A FEW HERE)
....
....
....

GIFT (WRITE ABOUT WHAT LIFE WOULD LIKE BE IF YOU FOLLOW THE WORD)
....

CHOICE (YOU HAVE FREE WILL, WRITE OUT HOW YOU PLAN TO FOLLOW THROUGH)
....

MEDITATION *Verse*

(REWRITE YESTERDAY'S PROBLEM-WORD-GIFT-CHOICE MEMORY VERSE HERE)

Date: _____

| S | M | T | W | T | F | S |

MEALS:

BREAKFAST

LUNCH

DINNER

PRIORITIES:

☐ EXERCISED
☐ DEVOTIONS & JOURNAL COMPLETED

05:00
06:00
07:00
08:00
09:00
10:00
11:00
12:00
1:00
2:00
3:00
4:00
5:00
6:00
7:00
8:00
9:00

☐ PRAY FOR TODAY, HIS COVERING AS YOU SLEEP, AND HIS PRESENCE TOMORROW
☐ MOVE UNDONE TO-DO'S TO TOMORROW

WATER:
○ ○ ○ ○
○ ○ ○ ○

GOALS:

HOME:

SELF:

WORK:

TO DO:

☐
☐
☐
☐
☐
☐
☐
☐
☐
☐
☐
☐
☐
☐
☐
☐
☐

LAY DOWN YOUR *Sins*

LIFT UP YOUR *Wins*

Journal
RECORD NUDGES FROM DAILY DEVOTION

The Legacy Leaders like to use a popular process of P.R.A.Y. (pause, rejoice, ask, yield) after their daily Devo. As things come to you trust that it is the Holy Spirit nudging you and then do PROBLEM/WORD/GIFT/CHOICE to tap into God's help.

FREE JOURNALING OF WHATEVER IS ON YOUR MIND AS YOU THINK, LISTEN, OR WHAT WEIGHS ON YOUR MIND:

....
....
....

P (PAUSE)
....

R (REJOICE)
....

A (ASK)
....

Y (YIELD)
....

WAS THERE ANYTHING YOU FELT NUDGED TO WORK ON? LET'S TAP INTO THE WORD FOR HELP

PROBLEM (EXAMPLES ARE WORRY, FEAR, DOUBT, INSECURITY, IMPATIENCE)
....

WORD (GO TO THE INTERNET & LOOK UP 'MEMORY VERSES ON YOUR TOPIC & RECORD A FEW HERE)
....
....

GIFT (WRITE ABOUT WHAT LIFE WOULD LIKE BE IF YOU FOLLOW THE WORD)
....

CHOICE (YOU HAVE FREE WILL, WRITE OUT HOW YOU PLAN TO FOLLOW THROUGH)
....

MEDITATION *Verse*

(REWRITE YESTERDAY'S PROBLEM-WORD-GIFT-CHOICE MEMORY VERSE HERE

Date: _____

| S | M | T | W | T | F | S |

MEALS:

BREAKFAST

LUNCH

DINNER

PRIORITIES:

- [ ] EXERCISED
- [ ] DEVOTIONS & JOURNAL COMPLETED

05:00
06:00
07:00
08:00
09:00
10:00
11:00
12:00
1:00
2:00
3:00
4:00
5:00
6:00
7:00
8:00
9:00

WATER:
○ ○ ○ ○
○ ○ ○ ○

GOALS:

HOME:

SELF:

WORK:

TO DO:

- [ ]
- [ ]
- [ ]
- [ ]
- [ ]
- [ ]
- [ ]
- [ ]
- [ ]
- [ ]
- [ ]
- [ ]
- [ ]
- [ ]
- [ ]
- [ ]

LAY DOWN YOUR *Sins*

LIFT UP YOUR *Wins*

- [ ] PRAY FOR TODAY, HIS COVERING AS YOU SLEEP, AND HIS PRESENCE TOMORROW
- [ ] MOVE UNDONE TO-DO'S TO TOMORROW

Journal
RECORD NUDGES FROM DAILY DEVOTION

The Legacy Leaders like to use a popular process of P.R.A.Y. (pause, rejoice, ask, yield) after their daily Devo. As things come to you trust that it is the Holy Spirit nudging you and then do PROBLEM/WORD/GIFT/CHOICE to tap into God's help.

FREE JOURNALING OF WHATEVER IS ON YOUR MIND AS YOU THINK, LISTEN, OR WHAT WEIGHS ON YOUR MIND:

....
....
....

P (PAUSE)
....

R (REJOICE)
....

A (ASK)
....

Y (YIELD)
....
....

WAS THERE ANYTHING YOU FELT NUDGED TO WORK ON? LET'S TAP INTO THE WORD FOR HELP

PROBLEM (EXAMPLES ARE WORRY, FEAR, DOUBT, INSECURITY, IMPATIENCE)
....

WORD (GO TO THE INTERNET & LOOK UP 'MEMORY VERSES ON YOUR TOPIC & RECORD A FEW HERE)
....
....
....

GIFT (WRITE ABOUT WHAT LIFE WOULD LIKE BE IF YOU FOLLOW THE WORD)
....

CHOICE (YOU HAVE FREE WILL, WRITE OUT HOW YOU PLAN TO FOLLOW THROUGH)
....
....

MEDITATION *Verse*

(REWRITE YESTERDAY'S PROBLEM-WORD-GIFT-CHOICE MEMORY VERSE HERE)

Date: _____

| S | M | T | W | T | F | S |

MEALS:

BREAKFAST

LUNCH

DINNER

PRIORITIES:

☐ EXERCISED
☐ DEVOTIONS & JOURNAL COMPLETED

- 05:00
- 06:00
- 07:00
- 08:00
- 09:00
- 10:00
- 11:00
- 12:00
- 1:00
- 2:00
- 3:00
- 4:00
- 5:00
- 6:00
- 7:00
- 8:00
- 9:00

☐ PRAY FOR TODAY, HIS COVERING AS YOU SLEEP, AND HIS PRESENCE TOMORROW
☐ MOVE UNDONE TO-DO'S TO TOMORROW

WATER:
○ ○ ○ ○
○ ○ ○ ○

GOALS:

HOME:

SELF:

WORK:

TO DO:
☐
☐
☐
☐
☐
☐
☐
☐
☐
☐
☐
☐
☐
☐
☐

LAY DOWN YOUR *Sins*

LIFT UP YOUR *Wins*

Journal
RECORD NUDGES FROM DAILY DEVOTION

The Legacy Leaders like to use a popular process of P.R.A.Y. (pause, rejoice, ask, yield) after their daily Devo. As things come to you trust that it is the Holy Spirit nudging you and then do PROBLEM/WORD/GIFT/CHOICE to tap into God's help.

FREE JOURNALING OF WHATEVER IS ON YOUR MIND AS YOU THINK, LISTEN, OR WHAT WEIGHS ON YOUR MIND:

....
....
....

P (PAUSE)
....

R (REJOICE)
....

A (ASK)
....

Y (YIELD)
....
....

WAS THERE ANYTHING YOU FELT NUDGED TO WORK ON? LET'S TAP INTO THE WORD FOR HELP

PROBLEM (EXAMPLES ARE WORRY, FEAR, DOUBT, INSECURITY, IMPATIENCE)
....

WORD (GO TO THE INTERNET & LOOK UP 'MEMORY VERSES ON YOUR TOPIC & RECORD A FEW HERE)
....
....
....

GIFT (WRITE ABOUT WHAT LIFE WOULD LIKE BE IF YOU FOLLOW THE WORD)
....

CHOICE (YOU HAVE FREE WILL. WRITE OUT HOW YOU PLAN TO FOLLOW THROUGH)
....

MEDITATION *Verse*

(REWRITE YESTERDAY'S PROBLEM-WORD-GIFT-CHOICE MEMORY VERSE HERE

Date:_____

| S | M | T | W | T | F | S |

MEALS:

BREAKFAST

LUNCH

DINNER

PRIORITIES:

- [ ] EXERCISED
- [ ] DEVOTIONS & JOURNAL COMPLETED

05:00
06:00
07:00
08:00
09:00
10:00
11:00
12:00
1:00
2:00
3:00
4:00
5:00
6:00
7:00
8:00
9:00

WATER:
○ ○ ○
○ ○ ○

GOALS:

HOME:

SELF:

WORK:

TO DO:
- [ ]
- [ ]
- [ ]
- [ ]
- [ ]
- [ ]
- [ ]
- [ ]
- [ ]
- [ ]
- [ ]
- [ ]
- [ ]
- [ ]
- [ ]
- [ ]
- [ ]

LAY DOWN YOUR *Sins*

LIFT UP YOUR *Wings*

- [ ] PRAY FOR TODAY, HIS COVERING AS YOU SLEEP, AND HIS PRESENCE TOMORROW
- [ ] MOVE UNDONE TO-DO'S TO TOMORROW

Journal
RECORD NUDGES FROM DAILY DEVOTION

The Legacy Leaders like to use a popular process of P.R.A.Y. (pause, rejoice, ask, yield) after their daily Devo. As things come to you trust that it is the Holy Spirit nudging you and then do PROBLEM/WORD/GIFT/CHOICE to tap into God's help.

FREE JOURNALING OF WHATEVER IS ON YOUR MIND AS YOU THINK, LISTEN, OR WHAT WEIGHS ON YOUR MIND:

....
....
....

P (PAUSE)
....

R (REJOICE)
....

A (ASK)
....

Y (YIELD)
....
....

WAS THERE ANYTHING YOU FELT NUDGED TO WORK ON? LET'S TAP INTO THE WORD FOR HELP

PROBLEM (EXAMPLES ARE WORRY, FEAR, DOUBT, INSECURITY, IMPATIENCE)
....

WORD (GO TO THE INTERNET & LOOK UP 'MEMORY VERSES ON YOUR TOPIC & RECORD A FEW HERE)
....
....

GIFT (WRITE ABOUT WHAT LIFE WOULD LIKE BE IF YOU FOLLOW THE WORD)
....

CHOICE (YOU HAVE FREE WILL, WRITE OUT HOW YOU PLAN TO FOLLOW THROUGH)
....

MEDITATION *Verse*

(REWRITE YESTERDAY'S PROBLEM-WORD-GIFT-CHOICE MEMORY VERSE HERE

Date: _____

| S | M | T | W | T | F | S |

MEALS:

BREAKFAST

LUNCH

DINNER

PRIORITIES:

☐ EXERCISED
☐ DEVOTIONS & JOURNAL COMPLETED

05:00
06:00
07:00
08:00
09:00
10:00
11:00
12:00
1:00
2:00
3:00
4:00
5:00
6:00
7:00
8:00
9:00

WATER:
○ ○ ○ ○
○ ○ ○ ○

GOALS:

HOME:

SELF:

WORK:

TO DO:
☐
☐
☐
☐
☐
☐
☐
☐
☐
☐
☐
☐
☐
☐
☐
☐

LAY DOWN YOUR *Sins*

LIFT UP YOUR *Wins*

☐ PRAY FOR TODAY, HIS COVERING AS YOU SLEEP, AND HIS PRESENCE TOMORROW
☐ MOVE UNDONE TO-DO'S TO TOMORROW

Journal

RECORD NUDGES FROM DAILY DEVOTION

The Legacy Leaders like to use a popular process of P.R.A.Y. (pause, rejoice, ask, yield) after their daily Devo. As things come to you trust that it is the Holy Spirit nudging you and then do PROBLEM/WORD/GIFT/CHOICE to tap into God's help.

FREE JOURNALING OF WHATEVER IS ON YOUR MIND AS YOU THINK, LISTEN, OR WHAT WEIGHS ON YOUR MIND:

....
....
....
....

P (PAUSE)
....

R (REJOICE)
....

A (ASK)
....

Y (YIELD)
....
....

WAS THERE ANYTHING YOU FELT NUDGED TO WORK ON? LET'S TAP INTO THE WORD FOR HELP

PROBLEM (EXAMPLES ARE WORRY, FEAR, DOUBT, INSECURITY, IMPATIENCE)
....

WORD (GO TO THE INTERNET & LOOK UP 'MEMORY VERSES ON YOUR TOPIC & RECORD A FEW HERE)
....
....
....

GIFT (WRITE ABOUT WHAT LIFE WOULD LIKE BE IF YOU FOLLOW THE WORD)
....

CHOICE (YOU HAVE FREE WILL. WRITE OUT HOW YOU PLAN TO FOLLOW THROUGH)
....
....

MEDITATION *Verse*

(REWRITE YESTERDAY'S PROBLEM-WORD-GIFT-CHOICE MEMORY VERSE HERE

Date: _____

| S | M | T | W | T | F | S |

MEALS:

BREAKFAST

LUNCH

DINNER

PRIORITIES:

☐ EXERCISED
☐ DEVOTIONS & JOURNAL COMPLETED

05:00
06:00
07:00
08:00
09:00
10:00
11:00
12:00
1:00
2:00
3:00
4:00
5:00
6:00
7:00
8:00
9:00

WATER:
○ ○ ○ ○
○ ○ ○ ○

GOALS:

HOME:

SELF:

WORK:

TO DO:
☐
☐
☐
☐
☐
☐
☐
☐
☐
☐
☐
☐
☐
☐
☐
☐
☐

LAY DOWN YOUR *Sins*

LIFT UP YOUR *Wins*

☐ PRAY FOR TODAY, HIS COVERING AS YOU SLEEP, AND HIS PRESENCE TOMORROW
☐ MOVE UNDONE TO-DO'S TO TOMORROW

Journal
RECORD NUDGES FROM DAILY DEVOTION

The Legacy Leaders like to use a popular process of P.R.A.Y. (pause, rejoice, ask, yield) after their daily Devo. As things come to you trust that it is the Holy Spirit nudging you and then do PROBLEM/WORD/GIFT/CHOICE to tap into God's help.

FREE JOURNALING OF WHATEVER IS ON YOUR MIND AS YOU THINK, LISTEN, OR WHAT WEIGHS ON YOUR MIND:

_____
_____
_____

P (PAUSE)
_____

R (REJOICE)
_____

A (ASK)
_____

Y (YIELD)
_____
_____

WAS THERE ANYTHING YOU FELT NUDGED TO WORK ON? LET'S TAP INTO THE WORD FOR HELP

PROBLEM (EXAMPLES ARE WORRY, FEAR, DOUBT, INSECURITY, IMPATIENCE)
_____

WORD (GO TO THE INTERNET & LOOK UP 'MEMORY VERSES ON YOUR TOPIC & RECORD A FEW HERE)
_____
_____
_____

GIFT (WRITE ABOUT WHAT LIFE WOULD LIKE BE IF YOU FOLLOW THE WORD)
_____

CHOICE (YOU HAVE FREE WILL, WRITE OUT HOW YOU PLAN TO FOLLOW THROUGH)
_____
_____

MEDITATION *Verse*

(REWRITE YESTERDAY'S PROBLEM-WORD-GIFT-CHOICE MEMORY VERSE HERE)

Date: _____

| S | M | T | W | T | F | S |

MEALS:

BREAKFAST

LUNCH

DINNER

PRIORITIES:

☐ EXERCISED
☐ DEVOTIONS & JOURNAL COMPLETED

05:00
06:00
07:00
08:00
09:00
10:00
11:00
12:00
1:00
2:00
3:00
4:00
5:00
6:00
7:00
8:00
9:00

☐ PRAY FOR TODAY, HIS COVERING AS YOU SLEEP, AND HIS PRESENCE TOMORROW
☐ MOVE UNDONE TO-DO'S TO TOMORROW

WATER:
○ ○ ○ ○
○ ○ ○ ○

GOALS:

HOME:

SELF:

WORK:

TO DO:
☐
☐
☐
☐
☐
☐
☐
☐
☐
☐
☐
☐
☐
☐

LAY DOWN YOUR *Sins*

LIFT UP YOUR *Wins*

Journal
RECORD NUDGES FROM DAILY DEVOTION

The Legacy Leaders like to use a popular process of P.R.A.Y. (pause, rejoice, ask, yield) after their daily Devo. As things come to you trust that it is the Holy Spirit nudging you and then do PROBLEM/WORD/GIFT/CHOICE to tap into God's help.

FREE JOURNALING OF WHATEVER IS ON YOUR MIND AS YOU THINK, LISTEN, OR WHAT WEIGHS ON YOUR MIND:

....
....
....

P (PAUSE)
....

R (REJOICE)
....

A (ASK)
....

Y (YIELD)
....
....

WAS THERE ANYTHING YOU FELT NUDGED TO WORK ON? LET'S TAP INTO THE WORD FOR HELP

PROBLEM (EXAMPLES ARE WORRY, FEAR, DOUBT, INSECURITY, IMPATIENCE)
....

WORD (GO TO THE INTERNET & LOOK UP 'MEMORY VERSES ON YOUR TOPIC & RECORD A FEW HERE)
....
....

GIFT (WRITE ABOUT WHAT LIFE WOULD LIKE BE IF YOU FOLLOW THE WORD)
....

CHOICE (YOU HAVE FREE WILL, WRITE OUT HOW YOU PLAN TO FOLLOW THROUGH)
....

MEDITATION *Verse*

(REWRITE YESTERDAY'S PROBLEM-WORD-GIFT-CHOICE MEMORY VERSE HERE)

Date: _____

| S | M | T | W | T | F | S |

MEALS:

BREAKFAST

LUNCH

DINNER

PRIORITIES:

☐ EXERCISED
☐ DEVOTIONS & JOURNAL COMPLETED

- 05:00
- 06:00
- 07:00
- 08:00
- 09:00
- 10:00
- 11:00
- 12:00
- 1:00
- 2:00
- 3:00
- 4:00
- 5:00
- 6:00
- 7:00
- 8:00
- 9:00

☐ PRAY FOR TODAY, HIS COVERING AS YOU SLEEP, AND HIS PRESENCE TOMORROW
☐ MOVE UNDONE TO-DO'S TO TOMORROW

WATER:
○ ○ ○ ○
○ ○ ○ ○

GOALS:

HOME:

SELF:

WORK:

TO DO:
☐
☐
☐
☐
☐
☐
☐
☐
☐
☐
☐
☐
☐
☐

LAY DOWN YOUR *Sins*

LIFT UP YOUR *Wins*

Journal
RECORD NUDGES FROM DAILY DEVOTION

The Legacy Leaders like to use a popular process of P.R.A.Y. (pause, rejoice, ask, yield) after their daily Devo. As things come to you trust that it is the Holy Spirit nudging you and then do PROBLEM/WORD/GIFT/CHOICE to tap into God's help.

FREE JOURNALING OF WHATEVER IS ON YOUR MIND AS YOU THINK, LISTEN, OR WHAT WEIGHS ON YOUR MIND:

P (PAUSE)

R (REJOICE)

A (ASK)

Y (YIELD)

WAS THERE ANYTHING YOU FELT NUDGED TO WORK ON? LET'S TAP INTO THE WORD FOR HELP

PROBLEM (EXAMPLES ARE WORRY, FEAR, DOUBT, INSECURITY, IMPATIENCE)

WORD (GO TO THE INTERNET & LOOK UP 'MEMORY VERSES ON YOUR TOPIC & RECORD A FEW HERE)

GIFT (WRITE ABOUT WHAT LIFE WOULD LIKE BE IF YOU FOLLOW THE WORD)

CHOICE (YOU HAVE FREE WILL, WRITE OUT HOW YOU PLAN TO FOLLOW THROUGH)

MEDITATION *Verse*

(REWRITE YESTERDAY'S PROBLEM-WORD-GIFT-CHOICE MEMORY VERSE HERE)

Date:_____

| S | M | T | W | T | F | S |

MEALS:

BREAKFAST

LUNCH

DINNER

PRIORITIES:

- [ ] EXERCISED
- [ ] DEVOTIONS & JOURNAL COMPLETED

05:00
06:00
07:00
08:00
09:00
10:00
11:00
12:00
1:00
2:00
3:00
4:00
5:00
6:00
7:00
8:00
9:00

WATER:
○ ○ ○
○ ○ ○

GOALS:

HOME:

SELF:

WORK:

TO DO:
- [ ]
- [ ]
- [ ]
- [ ]
- [ ]
- [ ]
- [ ]
- [ ]
- [ ]
- [ ]
- [ ]
- [ ]
- [ ]
- [ ]
- [ ]
- [ ]

LAY DOWN YOUR *Sins*

LIFT UP YOUR *Wins*

- [ ] PRAY FOR TODAY, HIS COVERING AS YOU SLEEP, AND HIS PRESENCE TOMORROW
- [ ] MOVE UNDONE TO-DO'S TO TOMORROW

Journal
RECORD NUDGES FROM DAILY DEVOTION

The Legacy Leaders like to use a popular process of P.R.A.Y. (pause, rejoice, ask, yield) after their daily Devo. As things come to you trust that it is the Holy Spirit nudging you and then do PROBLEM/WORD/GIFT/CHOICE to tap into God's help.

FREE JOURNALING OF WHATEVER IS ON YOUR MIND AS YOU THINK, LISTEN, OR WHAT WEIGHS ON YOUR MIND:

....
....
....

P (PAUSE)
....

R (REJOICE)
....

A (ASK)
....
....

Y (YIELD)
....
....

WAS THERE ANYTHING YOU FELT NUDGED TO WORK ON? LET'S TAP INTO THE WORD FOR HELP

PROBLEM (EXAMPLES ARE WORRY, FEAR, DOUBT, INSECURITY, IMPATIENCE)
....

WORD (GO TO THE INTERNET & LOOK UP 'MEMORY VERSES ON YOUR TOPIC & RECORD A FEW HERE)
....
....
....

GIFT (WRITE ABOUT WHAT LIFE WOULD LIKE BE IF YOU FOLLOW THE WORD)
....

CHOICE (YOU HAVE FREE WILL, WRITE OUT HOW YOU PLAN TO FOLLOW THROUGH)
....

MEDITATION *Verse*

Date: _____

| S | M | T | W | T | F | S |

(REWRITE YESTERDAY'S PROBLEM-WORD-GIFT-CHOICE MEMORY VERSE HERE)

MEALS:

BREAKFAST

LUNCH

DINNER

PRIORITIES:

☐ EXERCISED
☐ DEVOTIONS & JOURNAL COMPLETED

05:00
06:00
07:00
08:00
09:00
10:00
11:00
12:00
1:00
2:00
3:00
4:00
5:00
6:00
7:00
8:00
9:00

WATER:
○ ○ ○ ○
○ ○ ○ ○

GOALS:

HOME:

SELF:

WORK:

TO DO:
☐
☐
☐
☐
☐
☐
☐
☐
☐
☐
☐
☐
☐
☐
☐
☐
☐

LAY DOWN YOUR *Sins*

LIFT UP YOUR *Wins*

☐ PRAY FOR TODAY, HIS COVERING AS YOU SLEEP, AND HIS PRESENCE TOMORROW
☐ MOVE UNDONE TO-DO'S TO TOMORROW

Journal
RECORD NUDGES FROM DAILY DEVOTION

The Legacy Leaders like to use a popular process of P.R.A.Y. (pause, rejoice, ask, yield) after their daily Devo. As things come to you trust that it is the Holy Spirit nudging you and then do PROBLEM/WORD/GIFT/CHOICE to tap into God's help.

FREE JOURNALING OF WHATEVER IS ON YOUR MIND AS YOU THINK, LISTEN, OR WHAT WEIGHS ON YOUR MIND:

P (PAUSE)

R (REJOICE)

A (ASK)

Y (YIELD)

WAS THERE ANYTHING YOU FELT NUDGED TO WORK ON? LET'S TAP INTO THE WORD FOR HELP

PROBLEM (EXAMPLES ARE WORRY, FEAR, DOUBT, INSECURITY, IMPATIENCE)

WORD (GO TO THE INTERNET & LOOK UP 'MEMORY VERSES ON YOUR TOPIC & RECORD A FEW HERE)

GIFT (WRITE ABOUT WHAT LIFE WOULD LIKE BE IF YOU FOLLOW THE WORD)

CHOICE (YOU HAVE FREE WILL, WRITE OUT HOW YOU PLAN TO FOLLOW THROUGH)

MEDITATION *Verse*

(REWRITE YESTERDAY'S PROBLEM-WORD-GIFT-CHOICE MEMORY VERSE HERE)

Date: _____

| S | M | T | W | T | F | S |

MEALS:

BREAKFAST

LUNCH

DINNER

PRIORITIES:

☐ EXERCISED
☐ DEVOTIONS & JOURNAL COMPLETED

- 05:00
- 06:00
- 07:00
- 08:00
- 09:00
- 10:00
- 11:00
- 12:00
- 1:00
- 2:00
- 3:00
- 4:00
- 5:00
- 6:00
- 7:00
- 8:00
- 9:00

☐ PRAY FOR TODAY, HIS COVERING AS YOU SLEEP, AND HIS PRESENCE TOMORROW
☐ MOVE UNDONE TO-DO'S TO TOMORROW

WATER:
○ ○ ○ ○
○ ○ ○ ○

GOALS:

HOME:

SELF:

WORK:

TO DO:

☐
☐
☐
☐
☐
☐
☐
☐
☐
☐
☐
☐
☐
☐
☐

LAY DOWN YOUR *Sins*

LIFT UP YOUR *Wins*

Journal
RECORD NUDGES FROM DAILY DEVOTION

The Legacy Leaders like to use a popular process of P.R.A.Y. (pause, rejoice, ask, yield) after their daily Devo. As things come to you trust that it is the Holy Spirit nudging you and then do PROBLEM/WORD/GIFT/CHOICE to tap into God's help.

FREE JOURNALING OF WHATEVER IS ON YOUR MIND AS YOU THINK, LISTEN, OR WHAT WEIGHS ON YOUR MIND:
....
....
....

P (PAUSE)
....

R (REJOICE)
....

A (ASK)
....

Y (YIELD)
....
....

WAS THERE ANYTHING YOU FELT NUDGED TO WORK ON? LET'S TAP INTO THE WORD FOR HELP

PROBLEM (EXAMPLES ARE WORRY, FEAR, DOUBT, INSECURITY, IMPATIENCE)
....

WORD (GO TO THE INTERNET & LOOK UP 'MEMORY VERSES ON YOUR TOPIC & RECORD A FEW HERE)
....
....
....

GIFT (WRITE ABOUT WHAT LIFE WOULD LIKE BE IF YOU FOLLOW THE WORD)
....

CHOICE (YOU HAVE FREE WILL, WRITE OUT HOW YOU PLAN TO FOLLOW THROUGH)
....

MEDITATION *Verse*

(REWRITE YESTERDAY'S PROBLEM-WORD-GIFT-CHOICE MEMORY VERSE HERE

Date: _____

| S | M | T | W | T | F | S |

MEALS:

BREAKFAST

LUNCH

DINNER

PRIORITIES:

☐ EXERCISED
☐ DEVOTIONS & JOURNAL COMPLETED

05:00
06:00
07:00
08:00
09:00
10:00
11:00
12:00
1:00
2:00
3:00
4:00
5:00
6:00
7:00
8:00
9:00

WATER:
○ ○ ○
○ ○ ○

GOALS:

HOME:

SELF:

WORK:

TO DO:
☐
☐
☐
☐
☐
☐
☐
☐
☐
☐
☐
☐
☐
☐
☐
☐

LAY DOWN YOUR *Sins*

LIFT UP YOUR *Wins*

☐ PRAY FOR TODAY, HIS COVERING AS YOU SLEEP, AND HIS PRESENCE TOMORROW
☐ MOVE UNDONE TO-DO'S TO TOMORROW

Journal
RECORD NUDGES FROM DAILY DEVOTION

The Legacy Leaders like to use a popular process of P.R.A.Y. (pause, rejoice, ask, yield) after their daily Devo. As things come to you trust that it is the Holy Spirit nudging you and then do PROBLEM/WORD/GIFT/CHOICE to tap into God's help.

FREE JOURNALING OF WHATEVER IS ON YOUR MIND AS YOU THINK, LISTEN, OR WHAT WEIGHS ON YOUR MIND:

....
....
....

P (PAUSE)
....

R (REJOICE)
....

A (ASK)
....

Y (YIELD)
....
....

WAS THERE ANYTHING YOU FELT NUDGED TO WORK ON? LET'S TAP INTO THE WORD FOR HELP

PROBLEM (EXAMPLES ARE WORRY, FEAR, DOUBT, INSECURITY, IMPATIENCE)
....

WORD (GO TO THE INTERNET & LOOK UP 'MEMORY VERSES ON YOUR TOPIC & RECORD A FEW HERE)
....
....
....

GIFT (WRITE ABOUT WHAT LIFE WOULD LIKE BE IF YOU FOLLOW THE WORD)
....

CHOICE (YOU HAVE FREE WILL, WRITE OUT HOW YOU PLAN TO FOLLOW THROUGH)
....

MEDITATION *Verse*

(REWRITE YESTERDAY'S PROBLEM-WORD-GIFT-CHOICE MEMORY VERSE HERE)

Date: _____

| S | M | T | W | T | F | S |

MEALS:

BREAKFAST

LUNCH

DINNER

PRIORITIES:

- [ ] EXERCISED
- [ ] DEVOTIONS & JOURNAL COMPLETED

05:00
06:00
07:00
08:00
09:00
10:00
11:00
12:00
1:00
2:00
3:00
4:00
5:00
6:00
7:00
8:00
9:00

WATER:
○ ○ ○ ○
○ ○ ○ ○

GOALS:

HOME:

SELF:

WORK:

TO DO:

- [ ]
- [ ]
- [ ]
- [ ]
- [ ]
- [ ]
- [ ]
- [ ]
- [ ]
- [ ]
- [ ]
- [ ]
- [ ]
- [ ]
- [ ]

LAY DOWN YOUR *Sins*

LIFT UP YOUR *Wins*

- [ ] PRAY FOR TODAY, HIS COVERING AS YOU SLEEP, AND HIS PRESENCE TOMORROW
- [ ] MOVE UNDONE TO-DO'S TO TOMORROW

Journal
RECORD NUDGES FROM DAILY DEVOTION

The Legacy Leaders like to use a popular process of P.R.A.Y. (pause, rejoice, ask, yield) after their daily Devo. As things come to you trust that it is the Holy Spirit nudging you and then do PROBLEM/WORD/GIFT/CHOICE to tap into God's help.

FREE JOURNALING OF WHATEVER IS ON YOUR MIND AS YOU THINK, LISTEN, OR WHAT WEIGHS ON YOUR MIND:

P (PAUSE)

R (REJOICE)

A (ASK)

Y (YIELD)

WAS THERE ANYTHING YOU FELT NUDGED TO WORK ON? LET'S TAP INTO THE WORD FOR HELP

PROBLEM (EXAMPLES ARE WORRY, FEAR, DOUBT, INSECURITY, IMPATIENCE)

WORD (GO TO THE INTERNET & LOOK UP 'MEMORY VERSES ON YOUR TOPIC & RECORD A FEW HERE)

GIFT (WRITE ABOUT WHAT LIFE WOULD LIKE BE IF YOU FOLLOW THE WORD)

CHOICE (YOU HAVE FREE WILL, WRITE OUT HOW YOU PLAN TO FOLLOW THROUGH)

MEDITATION *Verse*

(REWRITE YESTERDAY'S PROBLEM-WORD-GIFT-CHOICE MEMORY VERSE HERE)

Date: _____

| S | M | T | W | T | F | S |

MEALS:

BREAKFAST

LUNCH

DINNER

PRIORITIES:

☐ EXERCISED
☐ DEVOTIONS & JOURNAL COMPLETED

- 05:00
- 06:00
- 07:00
- 08:00
- 09:00
- 10:00
- 11:00
- 12:00
- 1:00
- 2:00
- 3:00
- 4:00
- 5:00
- 6:00
- 7:00
- 8:00
- 9:00

WATER:
○ ○ ○ ○
○ ○ ○ ○

GOALS:

HOME:

SELF:

WORK:

TO DO:
☐
☐
☐
☐
☐
☐
☐
☐
☐
☐
☐
☐
☐
☐
☐
☐

LAY DOWN YOUR *Sins*

LIFT UP YOUR *Wins*

☐ PRAY FOR TODAY, HIS COVERING AS YOU SLEEP, AND HIS PRESENCE TOMORROW
☐ MOVE UNDONE TO-DO'S TO TOMORROW

Journal
RECORD NUDGES FROM DAILY DEVOTION

The Legacy Leaders like to use a popular process of P.R.A.Y. (pause, rejoice, ask, yield) after their daily Devo. As things come to you trust that it is the Holy Spirit nudging you and then do PROBLEM/WORD/GIFT/CHOICE to tap into God's help.

FREE JOURNALING OF WHATEVER IS ON YOUR MIND AS YOU THINK, LISTEN, OR WHAT WEIGHS ON YOUR MIND:

....
....
....

P (PAUSE)
....

R (REJOICE)
....

A (ASK)
....

Y (YIELD)
....
....

WAS THERE ANYTHING YOU FELT NUDGED TO WORK ON? LET'S TAP INTO THE WORD FOR HELP

PROBLEM (EXAMPLES ARE WORRY, FEAR, DOUBT, INSECURITY, IMPATIENCE)
....

WORD (GO TO THE INTERNET & LOOK UP 'MEMORY VERSES ON YOUR TOPIC & RECORD A FEW HERE)
....
....
....

GIFT (WRITE ABOUT WHAT LIFE WOULD LIKE BE IF YOU FOLLOW THE WORD)
....

CHOICE (YOU HAVE FREE WILL, WRITE OUT HOW YOU PLAN TO FOLLOW THROUGH)
....
....

MEDITATION *Verse*

(REWRITE YESTERDAY'S PROBLEM-WORD-GIFT-CHOICE MEMORY VERSE HERE)

Date: _____

| S | M | T | W | T | F | S |

MEALS:

BREAKFAST

LUNCH

DINNER

PRIORITIES:
- [ ] EXERCISED
- [ ] DEVOTIONS & JOURNAL COMPLETED

05:00
06:00
07:00
08:00
09:00
10:00
11:00
12:00
1:00
2:00
3:00
4:00
5:00
6:00
7:00
8:00
9:00

- [ ] PRAY FOR TODAY, HIS COVERING AS YOU SLEEP, AND HIS PRESENCE TOMORROW
- [ ] MOVE UNDONE TO-DO'S TO TOMORROW

WATER:
○ ○ ○
○ ○ ○

GOALS:

HOME:

SELF:

WORK:

TO DO:
- [ ]
- [ ]
- [ ]
- [ ]
- [ ]
- [ ]
- [ ]
- [ ]
- [ ]
- [ ]
- [ ]
- [ ]
- [ ]
- [ ]

LAY DOWN YOUR *Sins*

LIFT UP YOUR *Wins*

Journal
RECORD NUDGES FROM DAILY DEVOTION

The Legacy Leaders like to use a popular process of P.R.A.Y. (pause, rejoice, ask, yield) after their daily Devo. As things come to you trust that it is the Holy Spirit nudging you and then do PROBLEM/WORD/GIFT/CHOICE to tap into God's help.

FREE JOURNALING OF WHATEVER IS ON YOUR MIND AS YOU THINK, LISTEN, OR WHAT WEIGHS ON YOUR MIND:

....
....
....

P (PAUSE)
....

R (REJOICE)
....

A (ASK)
....

Y (YIELD)
....
....

WAS THERE ANYTHING YOU FELT NUDGED TO WORK ON? LET'S TAP INTO THE WORD FOR HELP

PROBLEM (EXAMPLES ARE WORRY, FEAR, DOUBT, INSECURITY, IMPATIENCE)
....

WORD (GO TO THE INTERNET & LOOK UP 'MEMORY VERSES ON YOUR TOPIC & RECORD A FEW HERE)
....
....
....

GIFT (WRITE ABOUT WHAT LIFE WOULD LIKE BE IF YOU FOLLOW THE WORD)
....

CHOICE (YOU HAVE FREE WILL, WRITE OUT HOW YOU PLAN TO FOLLOW THROUGH)
....

MEDITATION *Verse*

(REWRITE YESTERDAY'S PROBLEM-WORD-GIFT-CHOICE MEMORY VERSE HERE)

Date: _____

| S | M | T | W | T | F | S |

MEALS:

BREAKFAST

LUNCH

DINNER

PRIORITIES:

☐ EXERCISED
☐ DEVOTIONS & JOURNAL COMPLETED

05:00
06:00
07:00
08:00
09:00
10:00
11:00
12:00
1:00
2:00
3:00
4:00
5:00
6:00
7:00
8:00
9:00

☐ PRAY FOR TODAY, HIS COVERING AS YOU SLEEP, AND HIS PRESENCE TOMORROW
☐ MOVE UNDONE TO-DO'S TO TOMORROW

WATER:
○ ○ ○ ○
○ ○ ○ ○

GOALS:

HOME:

SELF:

WORK:

TO DO:
☐
☐
☐
☐
☐
☐
☐
☐
☐
☐
☐
☐
☐
☐

LAY DOWN YOUR *Sins*

LIFT UP YOUR *Wins*

Journal
RECORD NUDGES FROM DAILY DEVOTION

The Legacy Leaders like to use a popular process of P.R.A.Y. (pause, rejoice, ask, yield) after their daily Devo. As things come to you trust that it is the Holy Spirit nudging you and then do PROBLEM/WORD/GIFT/CHOICE to tap into God's help.

FREE JOURNALING OF WHATEVER IS ON YOUR MIND AS YOU THINK, LISTEN, OR WHAT WEIGHS ON YOUR MIND:

....
....
....

P (PAUSE)
....

R (REJOICE)
....

A (ASK)
....

Y (YIELD)
....
....

WAS THERE ANYTHING YOU FELT NUDGED TO WORK ON? LET'S TAP INTO THE WORD FOR HELP

PROBLEM (EXAMPLES ARE WORRY, FEAR, DOUBT, INSECURITY, IMPATIENCE)
....

WORD (GO TO THE INTERNET & LOOK UP 'MEMORY VERSES ON YOUR TOPIC & RECORD A FEW HERE)
....
....

GIFT (WRITE ABOUT WHAT LIFE WOULD LIKE BE IF YOU FOLLOW THE WORD)
....

CHOICE (YOU HAVE FREE WILL, WRITE OUT HOW YOU PLAN TO FOLLOW THROUGH)
....

MEDITATION *Verse*

(REWRITE YESTERDAY'S PROBLEM-WORD-GIFT-CHOICE MEMORY VERSE HERE)

Date: _____

☐ S ☐ M ☐ T ☐ W ☐ T ☐ F ☐ S

MEALS:

BREAKFAST

LUNCH

DINNER

PRIORITIES:

☐ EXERCISED
☐ DEVOTIONS & JOURNAL COMPLETED

- 05:00
- 06:00
- 07:00
- 08:00
- 09:00
- 10:00
- 11:00
- 12:00
- 1:00
- 2:00
- 3:00
- 4:00
- 5:00
- 6:00
- 7:00
- 8:00
- 9:00

☐ PRAY FOR TODAY, HIS COVERING AS YOU SLEEP, AND HIS PRESENCE TOMORROW
☐ MOVE UNDONE TO-DO'S TO TOMORROW

WATER:
○ ○ ○
○ ○ ○

GOALS:

HOME:

SELF:

WORK:

TO DO:
☐
☐
☐
☐
☐
☐
☐
☐
☐
☐
☐
☐
☐
☐
☐
☐
☐

LAY DOWN YOUR *Sins*

LIFT UP YOUR *Wins*

Journal
RECORD NUDGES FROM DAILY DEVOTION

The Legacy Leaders like to use a popular process of P.R.A.Y. (pause, rejoice, ask, yield) after their daily Devo. As things come to you trust that it is the Holy Spirit nudging you and then do PROBLEM/WORD/GIFT/CHOICE to tap into God's help.

FREE JOURNALING OF WHATEVER IS ON YOUR MIND AS YOU THINK, LISTEN, OR WHAT WEIGHS ON YOUR MIND:

....
....
....
....

P (PAUSE)
....

R (REJOICE)
....

A (ASK)
....

Y (YIELD)
....
....

WAS THERE ANYTHING YOU FELT NUDGED TO WORK ON? LET'S TAP INTO THE WORD FOR HELP

PROBLEM (EXAMPLES ARE WORRY, FEAR, DOUBT, INSECURITY, IMPATIENCE)
....

WORD (GO TO THE INTERNET & LOOK UP 'MEMORY VERSES ON YOUR TOPIC & RECORD A FEW HERE)
....
....

GIFT (WRITE ABOUT WHAT LIFE WOULD LIKE BE IF YOU FOLLOW THE WORD)
....

CHOICE (YOU HAVE FREE WILL, WRITE OUT HOW YOU PLAN TO FOLLOW THROUGH)
....
....

MEDITATION *Verse*

(REWRITE YESTERDAY'S PROBLEM-WORD-GIFT-CHOICE MEMORY VERSE HERE)

Date: _____

| S | M | T | W | T | F | S |

MEALS:

BREAKFAST

LUNCH

DINNER

PRIORITIES:

☐ EXERCISED
☐ DEVOTIONS & JOURNAL COMPLETED

05:00
06:00
07:00
08:00
09:00
10:00
11:00
12:00
1:00
2:00
3:00
4:00
5:00
6:00
7:00
8:00
9:00

☐ PRAY FOR TODAY, HIS COVERING AS YOU SLEEP, AND HIS PRESENCE TOMORROW
☐ MOVE UNDONE TO-DO'S TO TOMORROW

WATER:
○ ○ ○
○ ○ ○

GOALS:

HOME:

SELF:

WORK:

TO DO:
☐
☐
☐
☐
☐
☐
☐
☐
☐
☐
☐
☐
☐

LAY DOWN YOUR *Sins*

LIFT UP YOUR *Wins*

Journal
RECORD NUDGES FROM DAILY DEVOTION

The Legacy Leaders like to use a popular process of P.R.A.Y. (pause, rejoice, ask, yield) after their daily Devo. As things come to you trust that it is the Holy Spirit nudging you and then do PROBLEM/WORD/GIFT/CHOICE to tap into God's help.

FREE JOURNALING OF WHATEVER IS ON YOUR MIND AS YOU THINK, LISTEN, OR WHAT WEIGHS ON YOUR MIND:

....
....
....

P (PAUSE)
....

R (REJOICE)
....

A (ASK)
....

Y (YIELD)
....
....

WAS THERE ANYTHING YOU FELT NUDGED TO WORK ON? LET'S TAP INTO THE WORD FOR HELP

PROBLEM (EXAMPLES ARE WORRY, FEAR, DOUBT, INSECURITY, IMPATIENCE)
....

WORD (GO TO THE INTERNET & LOOK UP 'MEMORY VERSES ON YOUR TOPIC & RECORD A FEW HERE)
....
....

GIFT (WRITE ABOUT WHAT LIFE WOULD LIKE BE IF YOU FOLLOW THE WORD)
....

CHOICE (YOU HAVE FREE WILL, WRITE OUT HOW YOU PLAN TO FOLLOW THROUGH)
....

MEDITATION *Verse*

(REWRITE YESTERDAY'S PROBLEM-WORD-GIFT-CHOICE MEMORY VERSE HERE)

Date: _____

| S | M | T | W | T | F | S |

MEALS:

BREAKFAST

LUNCH

DINNER

PRIORITIES:

- [ ] EXERCISED
- [ ] DEVOTIONS & JOURNAL COMPLETED

05:00
06:00
07:00
08:00
09:00
10:00
11:00
12:00
1:00
2:00
3:00
4:00
5:00
6:00
7:00
8:00
9:00

- [ ] PRAY FOR TODAY, HIS COVERING AS YOU SLEEP, AND HIS PRESENCE TOMORROW
- [ ] MOVE UNDONE TO-DO'S TO TOMORROW

WATER:
○ ○ ○ ○
○ ○ ○ ○

GOALS:

HOME:

SELF:

WORK:

TO DO:
- [ ]
- [ ]
- [ ]
- [ ]
- [ ]
- [ ]
- [ ]
- [ ]
- [ ]
- [ ]
- [ ]
- [ ]
- [ ]
- [ ]
- [ ]
- [ ]
- [ ]

LAY DOWN YOUR *Sins*

LIFT UP YOUR *Wins*

Journal
RECORD NUDGES FROM DAILY DEVOTION

The Legacy Leaders like to use a popular process of P.R.A.Y. (pause, rejoice, ask, yield) after their daily Devo. As things come to you trust that it is the Holy Spirit nudging you and then do PROBLEM/WORD/GIFT/CHOICE to tap into God's help.

FREE JOURNALING OF WHATEVER IS ON YOUR MIND AS YOU THINK, LISTEN, OR WHAT WEIGHS ON YOUR MIND:

....
....
....
....

P (PAUSE)
....

R (REJOICE)
....

A (ASK)
....

Y (YIELD)
....
....

WAS THERE ANYTHING YOU FELT NUDGED TO WORK ON? LET'S TAP INTO THE WORD FOR HELP

PROBLEM (EXAMPLES ARE WORRY, FEAR, DOUBT, INSECURITY, IMPATIENCE)
....

WORD (GO TO THE INTERNET & LOOK UP 'MEMORY VERSES ON YOUR TOPIC & RECORD A FEW HERE)
....
....
....

GIFT (WRITE ABOUT WHAT LIFE WOULD LIKE BE IF YOU FOLLOW THE WORD)
....

CHOICE (YOU HAVE FREE WILL, WRITE OUT HOW YOU PLAN TO FOLLOW THROUGH)
....
....

MEDITATION *Verse*

(REWRITE YESTERDAY'S PROBLEM-WORD-GIFT-CHOICE MEMORY VERSE HERE)

Date: _____

| S | M | T | W | T | F | S |

MEALS:

BREAKFAST

LUNCH

DINNER

PRIORITIES:

☐ EXERCISED
☐ DEVOTIONS & JOURNAL COMPLETED

05:00
06:00
07:00
08:00
09:00
10:00
11:00
12:00
1:00
2:00
3:00
4:00
5:00
6:00
7:00
8:00
9:00

☐ PRAY FOR TODAY, HIS COVERING AS YOU SLEEP, AND HIS PRESENCE TOMORROW
☐ MOVE UNDONE TO-DO'S TO TOMORROW

WATER:
○ ○ ○ ○
○ ○ ○ ○

GOALS:

HOME:

SELF:

WORK:

TO DO:
☐
☐
☐
☐
☐
☐
☐
☐
☐
☐
☐
☐
☐
☐

LAY DOWN YOUR *Sins*

LIFT UP YOUR *Wins*

RECORD NUDGES FROM DAILY DEVOTION *Journal*

The Legacy Leaders like to use a popular process of P.R.A.Y. (pause, rejoice, ask, yield) after their daily Devo. As things come to you trust that it is the Holy Spirit nudging you and then do PROBLEM/WORD/GIFT/CHOICE to tap into God's help.

FREE JOURNALING OF WHATEVER IS ON YOUR MIND AS YOU THINK, LISTEN, OR WHAT WEIGHS ON YOUR MIND:

....
....
....

P (PAUSE)
....

R (REJOICE)
....

A (ASK)
....

Y (YIELD)
....
....

WAS THERE ANYTHING YOU FELT NUDGED TO WORK ON? LET'S TAP INTO THE WORD FOR HELP

PROBLEM (EXAMPLES ARE WORRY, FEAR, DOUBT, INSECURITY, IMPATIENCE)
....

WORD (GO TO THE INTERNET & LOOK UP 'MEMORY VERSES ON YOUR TOPIC & RECORD A FEW HERE)
....
....
....

GIFT (WRITE ABOUT WHAT LIFE WOULD LIKE BE IF YOU FOLLOW THE WORD)
....

CHOICE (YOU HAVE FREE WILL, WRITE OUT HOW YOU PLAN TO FOLLOW THROUGH)
....

05 *want to* LEARN MORE?

JOIN US IN THE LEGACY LEADER COMMUNITY. WE ELEVATE LIVES WITH THE POWER OF THE TRINITY. OUR GOAL IS TO GIVE YOU MORE OF WHAT YOU NEED — IN THE WAY GOD INTENDED. WE EACH TAKE UP OUR SEAT IN THE AREA HE HAS CALLED AND GIFTED US — SO WE CAN MORE ABUNDANTLY LIVE | LOVE | LEARN | LEAD ACCORDING TO THE CALL GOD HAS ON YOUR LIFE.

SIGN UP, FREE!

LEGACYLEADERCOMMUNITY.COM

www.ingramcontent.com/pod-product-compliance
Lightning Source LLC
Chambersburg PA
CBHW070423120526
44590CB00014B/1512